The Cambridge Introductio
Samuel Beckett

This book is an eloquent and accessible introduction to one of the most important writers of the twentieth century. It provides biographical and contextual information, but more fundamentally, it considers how we might think about an enduringly difficult and experimental novelist and playwright who often challenges the very concepts of meaning and interpretation. It deals with Beckett's life, intellectual and cultural background, plays, prose, and critical response and relates his work and vision to the culture and context in which he wrote. McDonald provides a sustained analysis of the major plays, including *Waiting for Godot, Endgame* and *Happy Days* and his major prose works including *Murphy, Watt* and his famous 'trilogy' of novels (*Molloy, Malone Dies, The Unnamable*). This introduction concludes by mapping the huge terrain of criticism that Beckett's work has prompted, and it explains the turn in recent years to understanding Beckett within his historical context.

RÓNÁN McDONALD is a Lecturer in English at the University of Reading and the Director of the Beckett International Foundation.

Cambridge Introductions to Literature

This series is designed to introduce students to key topics and authors. Accessible and lively, these introductions will also appeal to readers who want to broaden their understanding of the books and authors they enjoy.

- Ideal for students, teachers, and lecturers
- Concise, yet packed with essential information
- Key suggestions for further reading

Titles in this series:

The Cambridge Introduction to
Samuel Beckett

RÓNÁN McDONALD

CAMBRIDGE
UNIVERSITY PRESS

CAMBRIDGE UNIVERSITY PRESS
Cambridge, New York, Melbourne, Madrid, Cape Town, Singapore, São Paulo

CAMBRIDGE UNIVERSITY PRESS
The Edinburgh Building, Cambridge CB2 2RU, UK

Published in the United States of America by Cambridge University Press, New York

www.cambridge.org
Information on this title: www.cambridge.org/9780521547383

First published 2006

Printed in the United Kingdom at the University Press, Cambridge

A catalogue record for this publication is available from the British Library

Library of Congress Cataloguing in Publication data

ISBN-13 978-0-521-83856-6 hardback
ISBN-10 0-521-83856-8 hardback
ISBN-13 978-0-521-54738-3 paperback
ISBN-10 0-521-54738-5 paperback

For Sarah Montgomery

Contents

Chapter 5 Beckett criticism   116

Acknowledgements

I would like to thank my editor at Cambridge, Ray Ryan, for commissioning this book and for his advice during its composition. I was fortunate to have an accomplished Beckettian, David Watson, as an informed and helpful copy-editor. Like all who write on Beckett, I am in the debt of James Knowlson and John Pilling and am privileged to have had them as my colleagues at the Beckett International Foundation. I would like to thank Mark Nixon for reading and commenting on the manuscript. My greatest debt is reflected in the dedication. Responsibility for any errors in fact or interpretation remains my own.

Note on editions

Page numbers are cited parenthetically throughout. They are from the following editions.

Fiction

More Pricks than Kicks (London: John Calder, 1970)
Murphy (London: John Calder, 1963)
Watt (London: John Calder, 1963)
The Beckett Trilogy: Molloy, Malone Dies, The Unnamable (London: Pan, 1979)
How It Is (London: John Calder, 1964)

Drama

Waiting for Godot (London: Faber and Faber, 1965)
Endgame, followed by *Act Without Words* (London: Faber and Faber, 1958)
Happy Days (London: Faber and Faber, 1962)
All other plays from *Collected Shorter Plays* (London: Faber and Faber, 1984)

Criticism and Miscellaneous

Proust and Three Dialogues with Georges Duthuit (London: John Calder, 1965). Abbreviated P, followed by page number.
Disjecta, Miscellaneous Writings and a Dramatic Fragment, ed. Ruby Cohn (London: John Calder, 1983). Abbreviated D, followed by page number.

Introduction

'I'd be quite incapable of writing a critical introduction to my own works.'[1]

A generation after his death, Samuel Beckett remains one of the giants of twentieth-century literature and drama. More troubling for his critics, he is also one of the last century's most potent literary myths. Like other 'modernists', he has a reputation for obscurity and difficulty, yet despite this his work permeates our culture in unique ways. The word 'Beckettian' resonates even amongst those who know little Beckett. It evokes a bleak vision of life leavened by mordant humour: derelict tramps on a bare stage waiting desperately for nothing, a legless old couple peering out of dustbins, geriatric narrators babbling out their final incoherent mumblings. It evokes sparseness and minimalism and, with them, a forensic, pitiless urge to strip away, to expose, to deal in piths and essences.

Part of the reason that Beckettian images have seeped into popular culture is of course because of his peerless influence on post-war drama. His stage images have a visual and concrete dimension that the modernist poets and novelists arguably lack. One can visualise the spare Beckettian stage more easily than the poetic urban wasteland. Moreover his plays are not perceived as so forbiddingly highbrow that several have not become staples of repertory theatre. The Beckett 'myth' or 'brand' has been fuelled by two related phenomena: Beckett's refusal to offer any explication of his own work, his insistence that they simply 'mean what they say', coupled with his determined reclusivity (a horror of publicity that led his wife to greet news of his 1969 Nobel Prize for literature with the words 'Quelle catastrophe!'). If Beckett expected his silence to close down speculations about the 'man' behind the work, it was a forlorn hope. Rather it fed the mystery and aura that surrounded him, bolstering his image as the saintly artist, untainted by grubby self-promotion or by the coarse business of self-explication.

Moreover, the lack of specificity of his drama, the deracinated sets and absence of geographical or temporal certainty supported the idea, especially amongst Beckett's early critics, that his work had a universal import, that it articulated something fundamental and trans-historical about what life and human existence were all about. Where are these plays set? Who are these nameless narrators? The uncertainty of identification was interpreted as a badge of the archetypal or the elemental. His stripped stages or nameless narrators seemed shorthand for everywhere and everyone. 'Existentialist' concerns, so prominent in the fifties, were read into Beckett's work, at least so far as it was seen as a generally bleak and bleakly general view of human existence.

Paradoxically, at the same time as he is vaunted for expressing a 'timeless' human condition, Beckett is celebrated as the truest voice of a ravaged post-war world. The skeletal creatures and pared-down sets of his plays, or the aged, bewildered, agonised narrators of his novels, are regarded as the proper artistic expression of a world bereft of transcendent hope, without God, morality, value or even the solace of a stable selfhood. Notwithstanding Theodor Adorno's declaration on the impossibility of art after Auschwitz, Beckett comes closest to being the laureate of twentieth-century desolation.

Whether of all time or of his own time, Beckett, then, is sometimes given the role of a secular saint. His writings, though often confusing, are always regarded as profound, even visionary. Appropriately, Beckett's own, very striking face has entered modern iconography. Indeed there is no other writer of the post-war period whose face is so well known in comparison with his voice. It is always that of the older Beckett with his instantly recognisable, thin, angular countenance, furrowed with lines, the cropped grey hair, the long beak-like nose and, above all, those penetrating blue ('gull-like') eyes. The willingness to be photographed, coupled with the unwillingness to be interviewed, made him, ironically, one of the world's most recognisable recluses.

There is, then, a unique cult of veneration amongst Beckett's followers, imitators and devotees. Not only has he escaped the slump in popularity that afflicts a lot of writers in the years immediately after their death, but he also seems invulnerable to much of the critical backlash against some of the modernist writers over the past decade. A participant in the French Resistance and an opponent of totalitarianism in all its forms, Beckett was never going to merit the censure directed at some other modernist writers for anti-Semitism or reactionary political views. The Beckett myth, the aura of artistic integrity, elemental truth and existential bravery that surrounds him, is now something of which the vigilant Beckett reader needs to be wary. Reading Beckett, like (for all the differences) reading Shakespeare, means engaging with a complex web of cultural associations and literary prestige.

This book sets out to help the student, the theatre-goer, and the non-specialist general reader to think critically about Beckett and his major works. However, rather than simply providing answers or solving puzzles, this book strives to ask relevant questions. To engage fruitfully with Beckett's plays and novels does not necessarily mean to 'decode' them or to figure out what they really mean underneath the obscurity. One must heed the challenges they pose to the very acts of reading, viewing and interpretation. These are beautiful, crafted but thematically elusive plays and prose works. Readers or spectators are often drawn to Beckett, not because of some perceived idea or vision of life, but because of the compelling and utterly unique voice he has on stage and page. Beckett always put much more emphasis on the aesthetic qualities of his work than the meaning that could be extracted from them, on the shape rather than the sense. He once said, tellingly, 'The key word in my plays is "perhaps".'[2] In a very early critical essay on James Joyce he warned that the 'danger is in the neatness of identifications' (D 19). It is a warning which we should still heed.

Throughout the study of individual texts, I will try not just to dispel obscurity or difficulty, but also to ask what it is doing, how it functions aesthetically. While the source of an allusion or the occasional contextual gloss will from time to time be invoked, the primary intention of this book is not to provide annotation or explanation. As this book is intended as an introduction, references to other critics and secondary sources are kept to a minimum, outside the summary of criticism on Beckett provided in Chapter 5.

The Cambridge Introduction to Samuel Beckett is intended for people who have seen or read the works that are discussed herein and who want to think more about them. It will be of little use to someone who has not previously read the text under discussion. I have generally avoided providing plot summary or paraphrase of individual texts, not least to discourage students from adopting this approach in their own essays. Though this book can be read straight through, it may also be of use to a student who is doing a course that treats a single Beckett text – *Waiting for Godot* as part of a drama course, for instance – who will be able to consult the relevant section in this book.

Though I provide an overview of all Beckett's life and work in Chapter 1, this Introduction is *not* a comprehensive survey of all Beckett's plays and prose. The extended discussion of the works themselves in Chapters 3 and 4 focuses on the plays most often produced and the prose works most often read and studied, especially at undergraduate level. Unfortunately, this has necessitated omitting extended consideration of the minimalist skullscapes and dramaticules of Beckett's later period. These are rich, formally complex and intriguing texts, wholly resistant to summary. Rather than give the later works cursory or tokenistic treatment, I thought it preferable to omit them altogether from the extended critical readings. For the same reason, I have had to leave out critical consideration of Beckett's poetry, a lamentably neglected part of his oeuvre. This decision was made on the basis that more sustained treatment of individual difficult works would prove more useful to those encountering Beckett for the first time than stretching the space available to cover a sixty-year career more superficially.

Beckett expanded the possibilities of every form or literary mode he wrote in: short story, novel, stage play, radio play, film and television. When he started working in a new form or medium he learned the rules and grammar before fundamentally testing their limits. It is because his works are so inextricably attached to their mode, because the 'what' is so attuned to the 'how', that he was usually reluctant to allow adaptations. To illustrate this mastery, the intense sense that Beckett's work gives of probing the limits and possibilities of a medium, Chapter 3 includes a section on Beckett's radio plays, including an examination of *All That Fall* and *Embers*. *All That Fall* is one of the greatest radio plays ever written, and also, arguably, one of Beckett's most realist and accessible texts.

Finally, why are the plays before the prose, given that most of the novels treated were written before *Waiting for Godot*? There are a number of reasons for this sequence. First, Beckett is probably still better known as a playwright. While as a prose writer he is a key influence on such modern novelists as J. M. Coetzee and John Banville, his impact on post-war drama is unparalleled. The careers of Edward Albee, Harold Pinter, Tom Stoppard and countless others would be impossible to conceive without Beckett's influence. Many people encounter Beckett in the theatre and move on from his stage plays to read his novels. It is partly with this sequence in mind that the structure of this book is organised.

It is customary to think of 'difficulty' or 'obscurity' as being all about what we do not know. But Beckett proves that the experience of difficulty can come from simplicity as well as from complexity. He thwarts expectations not by bombarding us with new information, but by dispensing with familiarity, shattering assumptions and abandoning theatrical conventions. If the plays are, in general, more accessible than much of the prose, it is not just because of their concrete presence, their stark images that communicate viscerally, before the intellect has time to gauge their significance or meaning. It is also because of this radical and alienating *simplicity*. The difficulty of Beckett's early prose works – sardonic in tone and encrusted with erudition – is very different from that of his later drama, which makes theatre of minimal situations, or his later prose, so often based on repetition and variation of simple phrases and cadences. This is in one sense why Beckett always refused to offer explanations of what his plays might mean, insisting on the literal validity of what was on the page or stage. He wrote to Alan Schneider, his American director:

> I feel the only line is to refuse to be involved in exegesis of any kind. And to insist on the extreme simplicity of dramatic situation and issue. If that's not enough for them, and it obviously isn't, it's plenty for us, and we have no elucidations to offer of mysteries that are all of their making. My work is a matter of fundamental sounds (no joke intended) made as fully as possible, and I accept responsibility for nothing else. If people want to have headaches among the overtones, let them. And provide their own aspirin.   (D 109)

Chapter 1

Beckett's life

Samuel Beckett was a reluctant biographical subject. Though friends and acquaintances recollect a kind and generous man, he guarded his privacy with intense vigilance, seldom granting interviews and always claiming that his work should speak for itself. However, when his authorised biographer, James Knowlson, pointed out the recurrences of images from the Ireland of his childhood in his writing, he agreed. '"They're obsessional," he said, and went on to add several others.'[1] In early prose works, like *More Pricks than Kicks* (1934) or *Murphy* (1938), the correspondences of character and event with Beckett's own life are very explicit.[2] In his post-Second World War work, the biographical allusions become more submerged and less readily identifiable, just as the settings become more detached from a recognisable reality. Yet Beckett's imagination is saturated in his life experiences, even if the direct references to these experiences become rarer. Indeed, examination of the various drafts of Beckett's drama demonstrates what one critic has called the 'intent of undoing': the connections to a recognisable, and biographical, world become more attenuated as the drafts proceed.[3] The events in Beckett's life leave their traces in the shape of his work, without necessarily leaving an inventory in its content.

However, biographical criticism holds dangers too. Beckett is one of the most innovative and difficult writers of the twentieth century. It is tempting, faced with the often elusive meanings of his work, to seek refuge in ascertainable facts by pointing out correspondences with his life. The student of his work can then replace the task of interpretation with that of simple annotation – explaining the origins of a reference, an allusion, a character or an event, rather than asking what they might mean within the logic of the text. Finding the source of the stream will not by itself chart the river. Even if there is no absolute separation between Beckett's life and his work, neither should there be an absolute identification. The work will always produce meanings far in excess of its biographical or contextual annotations and, if we can find any coherence in Beckett's life, it should not be permitted to stand in for the incoherence and recalcitrance of his drama and prose.

It seems almost too good to be true that the twentieth century's most famous dramatist of suffering and desolation would be born on the day of the crucifixion but, sure enough, Samuel Barclay Beckett was born on Good Friday, 13 April 1906. He was the second son of William Frank Beckett, a successful quantity surveyor, and his wife Maria, known as May (née Roe) and was raised a Protestant in the affluent village of Foxrock, eight miles south of Dublin. Bill Beckett was a robust and kindly man whom Beckett loved very much. They would often go for long walks together in the Dublin and Wicklow hills, a topography and landscape found throughout Beckett's work, from *More Pricks than Kicks* through the trilogy to late works like *That Time* (1976) and *Company* (1980). The key to understanding Beckett, according to his friend and doctor Dr Geoffrey Thomson, was to be found in his relationship with his mother.[4] She was both loving and domineering, attentive and stern, and Beckett's love-hate relationship with her is at the crux of his intense feelings of anxiety and guilt. In later life he wrote of her 'savage loving',[5] and it seems his later decision to settle permanently in France was as much a flight from mother as from motherland. Even though Beckett claims to have 'no religious feeling', he acknowledges that his mother was 'deeply religious'.[6] The many biblical allusions in his work may partly derive from this influence. On being asked to describe his childhood, Beckett has called it 'Uneventful. You might say I had a happy childhood . . . although I had little talent for happiness. My parents did everything that they could to make a child happy. But I was often lonely.'[7] Loneliness, solitude, alienation would become recurrent themes in his later work.

As a member of the Irish Protestant minority in a largely Catholic country the young Beckett was something of an 'outsider', an experience which may have fed his later explorations of dislocated or marginal conditions. As the Anglo-Irish critic Vivian Mercier, musing on the similarity between his own background and that of Beckett, discerned:

> The typical Anglo-Irish boy . . . learns that he is not quite Irish almost before he can talk; later he learns that he is far from being English either. The pressure on him to become either wholly English or wholly Irish can erase segments of his individuality for good and all. 'Who am I?' is the question that every Anglo-Irishman must answer, even if it takes him a lifetime as it did Yeats.[8]

Perhaps this heritage of fractured identity, this search for the self, might have left its mark on Beckett's later preoccupation with a painful indeterminacy of subjectivity. 'Who am I?' is a question that Beckett's creatures repeatedly ponder. At the same time, however, we need to be wary of foreclosing or containing Beckett's complex and manifold probing of the nature of selfhood into a straight biographical correspondence. If his Irish Protestantism influences his later work, the implications and meanings of that work are certainly not limited to this source.

Moreover, we should be careful about unifying the identity of Irish Protestants into an undistinguished morass. We should not lump Beckett's cultural experience in with the 'Ascendancy', land-owning Protestant class to which J. M. Synge and Lady Gregory belonged and to which Yeats aspired. Beckett's was not a family that would have been comfortable in the literary salon. Though comfortably off and respectable, the family were not cultured or bookish, belonging rather to a high-bourgeois professional class. Hence, they were perplexed and worried when Beckett threw over a promising and respectable academic career for the insecurity of the Bohemian lifestyle and his mother kept the scandalously titled *More Pricks than Kicks* well out of sight of household visitors.

Importantly, this Protestant middle class, resident in the well-to-do Dublin suburbs, were more historically and politically insulated than their wealthier Ascendancy co-religionists. For Yeats and his collaborators art and literature were intimately associated with the 'nation'; indeed it was on these foundations that nationhood was formed. The resolutely middle-class and suburban milieu of Foxrock tended not to be so cultured or so politicised. This was not the land-owning class of the great Irish estates, whose social and political dominance had been undermined by the land reform of the last decades of the nineteenth century. It was class of professionals and bourgeois suburban self-containment, most of whose members commuted into the centre of Dublin every day to work. Therefore, though its instincts and allegiances would have been unionist and pro-British, the new dispensation after the Irish revolutionary period and the newly independent state after the treaty of 1921 had little effect on its day-to-day life. These large homes with long drives were at one remove from much of the violence and turmoil of Ireland's revolutionary period. There was little incentive or reason for this community to conceive of itself, or its privileges, in political terms.

Beckett, without obvious family precedent, became a great writer and intellectual. But it could be argued that the political insulation of his family background had a more enduring impact on his imagination. Beckett lived through extraordinary times from the start. His childhood and teenage years saw the rise of militant Irish nationalism and the subsequent War of Independence and Civil War. He was in Germany during the thirties and the consolidation of Nazi power, and in Paris during the occupation, where he joined the Resistance. However, there is another sense in which, until the Second World War, Beckett was cosseted and displaced from these 'interesting times'. The image of Beckett and his father, on a hill, miles outside Dublin, watching the flames rise during the Easter Rising of 1916, is a metaphor for his involvement in Irish politics at this time. Andrew Kennedy has said the boy and the young man were not 'subjected to the turmoil of war and revolution' and that 'it is the orderliness and the sheltered "old style" gentility of a pre-First World War childhood, at the relatively quiet edge of the Western world, that strikes one'.[9] There was, then, no need for someone of his background to think politically. It was not difficult for him, when he became a writer, to subscribe to that strand of cosmopolitan modernism which tended to disdain politically motivated art or cultural nationalism. His scornful attitude to the aims and ambitions of the Irish cultural revivalists, though presented as anti-provincialism, might also partly derive from the political immunity of his middle-class family background.

A young man 'with little talent for happiness', who nonetheless enjoyed a loving and cushioned upbringing, cannot find the causes of his misery in evidently temporal terms. So he finds the causes of unhappiness more readily in a pessimistic view of the world or in existence itself. Since the sources of unhappiness are not social or political, then, neither are the solutions to it. Hence his later dislike of political argument or discussion (even when he was touring Nazi Germany), such arguments striking him as pointless. 'There's a man all over for you,' exclaims Vladimir in *Waiting for Godot*, 'blaming on his boots the faults of his feet'(11).

Beckett went to private schools, first, Earlsfort House School in Dublin, then a boarding school, Portora Royal, in Enniskillen, the alma mater of Oscar Wilde. As well as his academic gifts, he gained a reputation for his athleticism and sporting prowess, particularly in rugby and cricket. In October 1923 he continued on the Wildean route to Trinity College Dublin, where he read French and Italian. After graduating in 1927, he spent an unhappy nine months teaching at the exclusive Campbell College in Belfast. When his dissatisfaction showed, he was asked by the headmaster if he realised that he was teaching the cream of Ulster society. 'Yes,' he replied, 'rich and thick.'[10] In November 1928, Beckett left Ireland for Paris, serving as teacher of English at the Ecole Normale Supérieure. There he became friends with the Irish poet and art critic Thomas MacGreevy, who became an intimate and confidant for many years. Their letters illustrate that Beckett, for all his great shyness and love of solitude, also needed friendship and intellectual companionship. MacGreevy introduced the young Beckett to literary society in the French capital, most importantly to James Joyce and his circle, including Eugene Jolas, the editor of the avant-garde, modernist magazine *transition*, which would publish some of Beckett's early work. Beckett was already familiar with the work of his fellow Dubliner, the revered author of *Ulysses* (1922) and an established titan of modernist literature. Though Joyce was a Jesuit-educated Catholic, Beckett shared much in common with the older man in terms of aesthetic and social outlook. Both came from middle-class families, both spurned the narrow cultural nationalism of the Irish Revival and both were passionately committed to the modernist and experimental literature of continental Europe. The influence was immense, and traceable not simply in terms of subject matter or literary style. Joyce became the vision of the artist as a figure of integrity, fulfilling his vocation with uncompromising dedication. Joyce's example taught the often indolent Beckett the importance of industry and application. It is from Joyce, too, that we can trace Beckett's determined resistance to all forms of censorship, of his own work or that of others, a conviction of the inviolate autonomy of the artist's intention that would later manifest itself in a refusal to countenance any altering or interference with his published work. Joyce's art always came first, and he never allowed the scruple of friends and family to prevent him from plundering autobiographical material for literary inspiration. Beckett's early prose works are full of a similar deployment of his own experiences in which, for example, his cousin Peggy Sinclair, with whom he had had his first love affair, is unflatteringly portrayed as the 'Smeraldina' in *More Pricks than Kicks* (a depiction he later came to regret).

But at the same time as Joyce showed the way, Beckett also realised that he had to find his own route. As Beckett told James Knowlson, 'I do remember speaking about Joyce's heroic achievement. I had a great admiration for him. That's what it was epic, heroic, what he achieved. But I realised that I couldn't go down that same road'.[11] For many writers, especially Irish writers, the influence of Joyce could be overwhelming. How could one ever emerge from so great a shadow? How could one find one's own voice when Joyce had, seemingly, so decisively sounded the limits of literary possibility? Later on, Beckett was certainly aware of the dangers and inhibitions of having the master in such close proximity. 'I vow I will get over J. J. ere I die. Yessir', he wrote to a friend in 1932.[12]

Beckett became a visitor at the Joyce household and occasionally helped the older man, whose sight was ailing, in his writing of 'Work in Progress' (known on its full publication as *Finnegans Wake* (1939)). He was subsequently invited to contribute to a collection of essays written by Joyce's friends to prepare the public for, and to generally promote, this most difficult and experimental of texts. Beckett's essay 'Dante . . . Bruno. Vico . . . Joyce' originally appeared in *transition* (1929), but would later be placed first in the collection entitled *Our Exagmination Round His Factification for Incamination of Work in Progress* (1929). But Beckett's visits to the Joyce home had an unexpected and unwelcome side effect, when he attracted the attentions of Joyce's daughter Lucia, whose incipient mental disturbance would later be diagnosed as schizophrenia. Her unreciprocated feelings would lead to a temporary rupture in Beckett's relations with the Joyce family.

Beckett was now a published writer with a connection to avant-garde literary circles in Paris. 'Assumption', his first published short story, also appeared in *transition* in 1929. The next year, his arcane poem 'Whoroscope', comically inspired by the life of Descartes and written quickly in order to enter a contest held by The Hours Press, won first prize. *Proust*, published in a series by Dolphin Press in 1931, was Beckett's first and only published critical study of any substantial length. Ostensibly an elucidation of Marcel Proust's masterpiece *A la recherche du temps perdu* (*In Search of Lost Time*) (1913–27), this short book is replete with philosophical ideas on time, habit, memory and so forth, ideas which bear the stamp of Beckett's own pessimistic intellectual disposition and his deep immersion in the nineteenth-century German philosopher Arthur Schopenhauer.

In autumn 1930, Beckett returned to Dublin to take up a post as a lecturer in French at Trinity College. There was every reason to hope for a brilliant academic career: the return for his parents' investment in his intellectual promise. However, Beckett's return to Dublin pushed him into great unhappiness, a psychological condition which – in an enduring affliction for Beckett – would manifest itself in physical illnesses. His relationship with his mother was, it seems, partly to blame for these ongoing disturbances. But he was not happy teaching either. This was partly because of the shyness that afflicted him all his life, but it was also because of his self-criticism, his refusal to distort or to misrepresent, a fidelity to the truth that we can trace into his artistic practice. He often said that he gave up his job because he 'could not bear teaching to others what he did not know himself'.[13] But despite the self-doubt and humility that this expression indicates, he was also repelled by the 'shallowness, paucity of interest and lack of literary sensitivity of most of those he was teaching'.[14] Probably this feeling underlay his rather more prosaic preference that he would rather lie on his bed and fart and think about Dante.

At the end of the autumn term 1931, on a visit to relatives in Germany, Beckett send back a letter to Trinity announcing his resignation. So began the 'vagabond years', a period of sustained peripatetic penury, as, travelling around Europe, he sought to establish himself as a writer. Friends and family felt both worried and betrayed, thus fuelling Beckett's own sense of guilt.

Here was a man in his late twenties, seemingly having abandoned an academic career, now directionless. After a short stay in Germany with Peggy Sinclair's family, he returned to Paris for six months, where he renewed his acquaintance with Joyce and wrote the bulk of his first novel, *Dream of Fair to Middling Women*, an ostentatious, highly erudite, fragmented and unconventional novel, dealing with the inner life and outer adventures of the Trinity student Belacqua Shuah, named after the indolent figure sheltering under a rock in Dante's *The Divine Comedy*. It failed to find a publisher and it was only posthumously published in 1992. But he would re-use much of it in *More Pricks than Kicks*.

After a disconsolate stint in London in summer of 1932, poverty forced him to crawl home to Dublin with 'my tail between my legs'.[15] Almost immediately he came into conflict with his mother. Health problems also began to plague him. The operation to remove a painful cyst on his neck in December 1932 would be the raw material for 'Yellow', one of the stories in *More Kicks than Pricks*. Two unexpected deaths later in 1933 exacerbated his despondency, guilt and depression. Lying in bed in May 1933, recovering from a recurrence of his suppurating neck, he learnt of the death of Peggy Sinclair from tuberculosis. On 26 June, his father died of a heart attack. 'I can't write about him,' he wrote to MacGreevy in his grief, 'I can only walk the fields and climb the ditches after him.'[16]

As well as his cysts and boils, Beckett's psychological condition resulted in frequent panic attacks and strong feelings of a racing heart. Seeking help for these disturbances, Beckett headed for London in later 1933 where he underwent psychotherapy with Wilfred Bion in the Tavistock Clinic. He submerged himself in books on psychology and psychoanalysis at this period and he also visited the Bethlem Royal Hospital, where an Old Portora school friend worked as a doctor. Much of the setting for the asylum scenes in *Murphy* and *Watt* (1953) come from these experiences, but the imprint of his personal experience of psychotherapy and his readings in psychoanalysis at this time is to be felt throughout his work. Much of it is cast in the form of a monologue in which a speaker, often lying on his back in dimness or dark, gabbles in a kind of delirium to a faceless listener.

More Pricks than Kicks appeared in 1934. The next year he published a slim volume of poetry, *Echo's Bones and Other Precipitates*. In need of money, and in contrast with his later critical silence, he wrote a number of reviews in literary magazines and an article acerbically criticising censorship and provincialism in Ireland. He started work on *Murphy* in August 1935 and completed it in June 1936. Beckett kept a list of the dozens of publishers who rejected his novel, and it was not published until Routledge took it on in 1938.

In 1936–7, Beckett toured Germany, spending much time in galleries and art exhibitions. During this time, he kept detailed diaries, which only came to light with Knowlson's biography. They testify to his eclectic reading in literature and philosophy at this intensely formative period and to his abiding interest in music and the visual arts. He made many notes on the various galleries he visited. The diaries are interesting, also, for what they tell us about Beckett's developing political sensibilities. While they record his distaste for Germany's increasing anti-Semitism and his scornful amusement at Hitler's interminable speeches, there is also some impatience and boredom with the anti-Nazi protests of some of his fellow artists. Admittedly Beckett could not foresee the horrors that Nazism would visit on Europe. But his attitude here betrays the same apolitical instincts that were incubated in his upbringing and later found confirmation in the modernist credo of literature as 'above' mere political concerns. What preoccupies Beckett at this stage is artistic expression in writing, music and painting, not the fleeting political ideologies of nationalism or National Socialism, which he views as ludicrous or distasteful, but not really something to which he should give his sustained attention. In a few years, it would be clear that politics could not be so easily bypassed or transcended.

He returned home to more friction with his mother, culminating in a terrible row later in 1937 which contributed to his resolution to leave Foxrock and Ireland for good. 'I am what her savage loving has made me,' he wrote to MacGreevy, 'and it is good that one of us should accept that finally.'[17] In addition to his general directionlessness and despondency, May Beckett was outraged by her son's involvement in a notorious literary court case in which Harry Sinclair (Peggy's uncle) had taken a libel action against the well-known writer-cum-medic Oliver St John Gogarty (himself immortally lampooned in James Joyce's *Ulysses* as 'Buck Mulligan'). Gogarty had given an anti-Semitic and unflattering depiction of the complainant's family in his memoir *As I Was Going Down Sackville St* (1937). Though the libel action was successful, and a disillusioned Gogarty retreated to exile in America, Beckett came out badly from the proceedings. The defence counsel's skilful attempts to discredit the prosecution's witness relied on depicting Beckett as a blasphemous and decadent 'intellectual' living in Paris, a byword for corruption by the rather censorious Irish standards of the time. Beckett fell for the bait, correcting his cross-examiner's deliberate mispronunciation of 'Proust' (had he written a book on 'Marcel Prowst'?). Asked if he was 'Christian, Jew or Atheist', Beckett responded, intriguingly, that he was none of the three. The damage was done. His mother was mortified by the public humiliation: the case was widely reported in the Dublin newspapers. Beckett was naturally shy and diffident anyway, but it may be that this unwelcome experience with the Dublin newspapers fuelled his later hostility to exposure and media attention. It certainly did nothing to help his attitude towards Irish provincialism and religious hypocrisy.

On 6 January 1938, Beckett was stabbed by a pimp on the Parisian streets for no obvious reason. The knife came very close to his heart. Friends and family rushed to his bedside, and he was reconciled with his mother. 'I felt great gusts of affection and esteem and compassion for her,' he wrote to MacGreevy. 'What a relationship!'[18] While he was recovering in hospital he was visited by a French woman whom he did not know well, but whom he had first met ten years previously, Suzanne Deschevaux-Dumesnil (1901–89). Though he was at the time involved with the American art patron Peggy Guggenheim, his relationship with Suzanne gradually supplanted this dalliance. He and Suzanne would remain together for the rest of their lives. Without her unstinting dedication to Beckett's genius, including her tireless attempts to find a publisher for his work, Beckett would probably never have achieved his success.

After the fall of France, Beckett came to feel the effects of war and invasion at first hand and to observe the treatment of his Jewish friends under Nazi occupation. The superciliousness of his earlier trip to Germany no longer seemed adequate. 'You simply couldn't stand by with your arms folded,' he later commented.[19] His friend Alfred Péron introduced him to a French Resistance cell, codenamed 'Gloria SMH'. At great personal risk, Beckett became actively involved in the Resistance in Paris, principally as an information handler. In August 1942, the cell was betrayed by a Catholic priest who was working for German intelligence. More than fifty members of 'Gloria SMH' were arrested and sent to concentration camps but, forewarned by Péron's wife, Beckett and Suzanne narrowly escaped and managed a hazardous journey to unoccupied France, where they lived out the rest of the war in Roussillon, a little village in the Vaucluse. Working as a farm labourer during the day, Beckett wrote his intriguing experimental novel *Watt* in the evening, a novel whose sense of entrapment and boredom possibly reflects the intellectually arid conditions of its composition. Predictably, there was difficulty after the war in finding a publisher willing to take a risk on a novel full of seemingly random permutations and combinations of words. It did not find a publisher until 1953. After the war, Beckett was decorated for his Resistance activities with the Croix de Guerre and the Médaille de la Reconnaissance Française. With characteristic self-deprecation he would later dismiss his wartime activities as 'Boy Scout stuff'.[20] Later in 1945, after a stint in Dublin, he returned to France by offering his services as an interpreter and storekeeper to the Irish Red Cross Hospital in Saint Lô before rejoining Suzanne in Paris.

There are few explicit references to the war in his work itself, but there is every sign that it deeply scoured his imagination. The intense confusion and atmosphere of persecution that haunts his later work, its population by nameless authority figures and inscrutable punishments, are crafted by a mind which had experienced the war first hand and indeed who had lost a number of friends in it. The war also seems to have contributed to a radical change of direction in his work. On a visit to his mother in Dublin, he had a 'vision' or a 'revelation' of literary purpose which marks the divide between his 1930s prose – third-person, erudite, controlled – and the dwindled, bewildered, first-person story-telling of the trilogy and beyond: '*Molloy* and the others came to me the day I became aware of my own folly. Only then did I begin to write the things I feel.'[21] Unlike some of his early writing, which shows the influence of Joyce in its word play and intertextual allusiveness, the post-war work carries its learning more lightly, making instead ignorance and impotence its key textual and thematic preoccupations. As he told Israel Shenker,

> The more Joyce knew the more he could. He's tending towards omniscience and omnipotence as an artist. I'm working with impotence, ignorance . . . My little exploration is that whole zone of being that has always been set aside by artists as something unusable – as something by definition incompatible with art.[22]

Abandoning the processes of assimilation, integration and allusion that Joyce had so resoundingly explored, Beckett strove instead for an art of disassembly, disintegration and ignorance. When the capacity to absorb or represent the external world dissolves, what is left is an immersive and inward-looking process. Beckett's mature style does not bombard us with styles or erudition, but comes to us as a voice from the darkness, a provisional consciousness uttering forth its own perplexity in bafflement and anguish.

Another important shift in his work after his 'revelation' was the decision to write in French (though he had written poems in French from the late thirties and had translated *Murphy* with Péron's help) in order to shake off the stylistic accretions and tics that he had accrued in English. His first novel in French, *Mercier et Camier*, was finished in 1946, and Beckett seems to have regarded it as an apprentice work. His refusal to allow it to be published until 1970 may partly be because it still has the 'externality' characteristic of some of his earlier prose works. However, treating two characters on a journey, its use of dialogue and verbal play prefigures his theatrical couplings in *Waiting for Godot* and *Endgame*. The same year he wrote four *nouvelles* that anticipate in theme and form the trilogy of novels that are now regarded as amongst his finest achievement. They show Beckett turning to the interior monologue as the form best suited to his new desire for self-excavation. His first full-length play in French was written at the beginning of 1947. *Eleutheria* was only published after Beckett's death and, to date, has never had a professional production. He was very determined that it would not be performed during his lifetime. While a flawed play, it contains many autobiographical elements in its treatment of a young man who refuses to come out of his room, in a desperate attempt to withdraw himself from his family and to achieve a degree of psychological freedom.

The work which would secure Beckett's place in the pantheon of great writers was penned, in French, in a 'frenzy of writing' between 1947 and 1950. In these years, when money was extremely scarce and his health ailing, he wrote, 'like a man freed from demons'.[23] His celebrated trilogy of novels, *Molloy* (1951, English version, 1955), *Malone meurt* (1951; *Malone Dies*, 1958) and *L'Innommable* (1953; *The Unnamable*, 1959), and his most famous play, *En attendant Godot* (1952; *Waiting for Godot* 1956), all come from this period. Though the 'trilogy' would come to be regarded as amongst the most important and innovative novels of the twentieth century, there was a familiar tale of rejection when it came to finding a publisher. Again, literary history owes a debt of gratitude to Suzanne, who, while sustaining Beckett and herself through her work as a dressmaker and music teacher, carried around the French manuscripts to dozens of publishers before finally, Jérôme Lindon of the Editions de Minuit became Beckett's French publisher.

What transformed Beckett from an avant-garde, experimental novelist to global stardom was *En attendant Godot*, written between October 1948 and January 1949 as a diversion from the more taxing (as he saw it) business of prose composition. Suzanne approached a French actor-director, Roger Blin, as did Lindon, and eventually enough money was raised to put on the play in a small Parisian theatre in January 1953. The play's success in Paris, and the international controversy it generated, prompted wide interest. It was put on all round Europe before it was finally produced in London in August 1955 (translated, as almost all his work, by Beckett himself) at the Arts Theatre Club under Peter Hall's direction. The initial reaction of the London audience and critics was scornful. As Peter Bull, who played Pozzo, recalled, 'Waves of hostility came whirling over the floodlights, and the mass exodus, which was to form such a feature of the run of the piece, started soon after the curtain had risen. The audible groans were also fairly disconcerting.'[24] However, when the respected reviewers Kenneth Tynan and Harold Hobson recognised the play's dramatic importance, it became an intellectual hit. Buoyed by the controversy it generated, *Waiting for Godot* would come to be hailed as the most revolutionary and influential play of the twentieth century.

Apart from the war years, Beckett spent at least a month a year every summer visiting his mother. Her decline and death from Parkinson's disease in 1950 caused him predictable anguish and guilt. With some money left him by her, Beckett purchased a house in Ussy-sur-Marne, outside Paris. He would come to describe this house as 'the house that Godot built' and it would become a haven for him for many years to come.[25] But despite the arrival of success, he was not to be spared more trauma and more grief. The decline and death from cancer of his brother Frank over the summer of 1954, which he witnessed first hand, was to sear itself onto his already scarred consciousness. The sense of loss, pain, ending and dread haunts *Fin de partie* (translated as *Endgame*) which he wrote later that year. The play was first put on in French, in London on 3 April 1957. It is an even darker play than its celebrated predecessor: the fellow-feeling amongst the two protagonists that in some way salved *Godot* was in much shorter supply here.

Beckett's prose follow-up to the trilogy, *Nouvelles et textes pour rien* (1955; *Stories and Texts for Nothing*, 1967), was a series of three short stories from 1946 and thirteen short prose fragments that, as the title indicates, were not highly regarded by Beckett. He felt in something of a logjam since his great outpouring of the late forties. In 1956 the Third Programme of the BBC commissioned Beckett to write a play, and the exploration of a new medium – the radio play – seems to have invigorated his creativity. The result, *All That Fall*, is one of the most autobiographical and overtly Irish plays of Beckett's career. It is as if he compensates for the non-material, ethereal radio medium by investing his play with compensatory geographical and historical ballast. The play is recognisably set in the Foxrock of his childhood. A later radio play, *Embers* (1959), though more ghostly and less clearly located than *All That Fall*, is also set on a beach in South Dublin and makes mesmerising use of the sound of falling waves and crushing shingle. His work with the BBC brought him into contact with Barbara Bray, a script editor there, with whom he would have a relationship, in parallel with that with Suzanne, for the rest of his life.

An atmosphere of death and the end of relationships characterised his next stage play, *Krapp's Last Tape* (1958), originally written for his favourite male actor, Patrick Magee (the play was to have been called *Magee Monologue*). With its use of recorded voices on stage, this play is clearly indebted to his forays into radio drama. In Beckett's first play of the 1960s, *Happy Days*

(1961), another theatrical image would sear itself onto dramatic history. In Act I its heroine, Winnie (this is the first of many Beckett plays with a female protagonist), is buried up to her waist in a mound of earth, in the second up to her neck, though her eloquent costumes and cheerful speeches comically contradict the (literal) gravity of her situation.

Beckett's initial move to drama was as a way of finding relief from the self-immersive and profoundly draining processes of his prose writings. These were, for him, his major expressive mode. After his novel trilogy, his next major prose text was *Comment c'est* (1961; *How It Is*, 1964). Dealing with a man crawling in the mud dragging a sack of canned food behind him, this 'novel' (if such is the term), is related in bursts of unpunctuated speech. It was to be Beckett's last extended prose work, though his later shorter works often continue the mode of unpunctuated utterance, providing glimpses of sparse, purgatorial landscapes.

In March 1961, Beckett secretly married Suzanne in England. The marriage seems to have been arranged hastily and mainly for testamentary reasons. Even though they were married, Beckett and Suzanne had developed a significant degree of autonomy. They had recently moved to a larger apartment in Paris and were there able to have separate bedrooms and separate hall doors. But this degree of separation should not be seen as indicative of an estrangement between the pair or as the beginnings of a separation. Rather it was a granting of space to each other. 'We simply must have our rooms where we can shut ourselves up,' Beckett had written to his friend Mary Manning Howe.[26] They were striving for a respectful space within marriage, a way of accommodating each other's independence.

After *How It Is*, Beckett's fiction took the form of what he called 'residua' or *têtes-mortes* (dead heads), becoming, like the plays, ever more condensed and minimalist. These texts, usually written first in French, include *Imagination morte imaginez* (1965; *Imagination Dead Imagine*, 1965), in which a man and a woman lie in the foetal position in a white, skull-like rotunda waiting for birth or extinction, *Assez* (1966; *Enough*, 1967), *Bing* (1966; *Ping* 1967), *Le Dépeupleur* (1971; *The Lost Ones*, 1972) and *Sans* (1969; *Lessness*, 1971). In these 'skullscapes' Beckett abandons the first-person narrative (with the exception of *Enough*) for a stripped down, quasi-mathematical impersonality, articulated in an unpunctuated, spare prose.

His plays of the sixties and seventies also tend towards the short and the formalist. In *Play* (1964) three speakers in urns are forced by a spotlight into rapidly telling the story of their adulterous liaison, the unconventionality of their situations parodying the deeply conventional and bourgeois relationships that their split narratives retell. Stage directions dictate that the language should be scarcely audible, as if situation and shape is more important than sense. In *Come and Go* (1967) three women take it in strictly ordered turns to leave the stage, giving the two remaining women the opportunity to commiserate on the terminal illness of the absent party. Its compressed, abstract, eerily symmetrical dramatic structure contrasts with the clichéd and worried confidences of the three women. It is a masterpiece of mordant humour. Their speech, as so much of Beckett's work in English, is heavily inflected with an Irish colouring.

Beckett's stature and the mystique surrounding him grew and grew, abetted rather than reduced by his persistent shunning of publicity. When he was awarded the Nobel Prize in 1969, he sent Lindon to Stockholm to accept the prize in his stead. During the sixties and seventies, Beckett became actively involved in the direction and production of his own work. In 1965, he worked on his film, entitled *Film*, starring Buster Keaton and directed by his American director friend Alan Schneider. He also wrote a play for television, *Eh Joe* (1967). In another significant chapter of his intriguing relationship with Germany, Beckett directed a series of his plays, principally at the Schiller Theatre in Berlin (though he also directed in Paris and London). In these productions, Beckett made many refinements and small adjustments to his original texts. Just as his plays become more and more precise, formal and symmetrical through his career, as a director he insisted on exact and prescribed movement from his actors. This is not a drama that communicates through vividness of emotion, but rather through highly stylised, mathematical movement and pacing. His dramatic work in the seventies continues his exploration of the female voice that first emerged in *Happy Days*. *Not I* (1973) was written for his favourite actress, Billie Whitelaw. Just as he heard the voice of Patrick Magee when writing *Krapp's Last Tape*, he heard her voice in writing this play. In another enduring Beckettian image, this play confines itself visually to a disembodied Mouth, illuminated from the darkness, eight feet above the stage. Whitelaw's performance under Beckett's direction is one of the great theatrical collaborations. But his search for formal stringency, a drama drained of warmth and colour the better to depict the cold and inhuman context within which the human person is trapped, meant that his direction of Whitelaw was tremendously prescriptive and restrictive. His demands on her were extreme in their scrupulous exactitude, but always couched courteously and gently. During rehearsals he would say, 'Too much colour, too much colour', which she correctly interpreted as 'For God's sake don't act.'[27]

In addition to *Eh Joe*, plays for television include '. . . *but the clouds*. . .' (1976), a haunting piece based on Yeats's The Tower, and *Ghost Trio* (1976), using Beethoven's music. Whitelaw would also go on to act in the stage play *Footfalls* (1976), another play with a female lead, who reflects distressfully on loss as she paces back and forward across the stage. *That Time* (1976), one of the most autobiographical of Beckett's works, is haunted with childhood memories. In this play the self is rent into three voices at different stages of life. *Ohio Impromptu* (1981) was given by Beckett to a conference devoted to him in Ohio. *Rockaby*, also first performed in 1981, treats a woman dressed in black rocking back and forwards in a rocking chair to the rhythm of her own recorded voice. Billie Whitelaw played the woman in its first production. In 1982, he wrote his most overtly political play, *Catastrophe*, for the imprisoned Czech dissident Václav Havel.

If *That Time* is his most autobiographical play, *Company* (1980), written in English, is the late prose work most coloured by childhood memories: the hedgehog he had shut up in a box, the diving at the 'Forty Foot' swimming place, falling from a tree in the garden. This text relies on third-person description of one who lies on his back in the dark and a second-person voice that remembers scenes from the past. *Mal vu mal dit* (*Ill Seen Ill Said*) (1981), written in French, features a woman narrator being drawn towards a white stone, resembling a tombstone, by twelve shadowy figures. It summons up a minimal scenario, an ill-seen image which is told by an ill-said narrative. *Worstward Ho* (1983), written in English, conjures up images of a woman, an old man, a child and a skull. It deals with depletion and value-inversion in various forms. *Stirrings Still* (1988) is Beckett's last prose text, although his final written work was a poem, 'Comment dire' or 'What is the Word' (1989).

Beckett's health began to decline seriously in 1986, with the onset of emphysema. He died in the Hôpital St Anne in Paris of respiratory failure on 22 December 1989, fewer than six months after Suzanne. After a small private funeral he was buried beside her in the cemetery of Montparnasse, Paris, on 26 December.

Chapter 2

Cultural and intellectual contexts

The problem with trying to locate Beckett in any national or cultural tradition is that, in his young days at any rate, he forswore any such relationship. He scorned an art which concerned itself with 'local accident' or the 'local substance', holding instead that the true object of literature is 'the issueless predicament of existence' (D 97). Take, for instance, his relationship with Ireland. His characters' names – Murphy, Molloy, Malone – and the cadence of their speech often have an Irish inflection while the topography of Beckett's childhood haunts his work. Yet he wrote most of his major works in French, before translating them, and spent most of his life abroad. Moreover, just as his early critical writing is impatient with politicised art, he has a great deal of scorn for cultural nationalism. He was clearly influenced by Irish forebears like Swift, Yeats and especially Synge but he had little time for the project of the Irish Revival that dominated cultural life in his native city while he lived there. In his 1934 essay 'Recent Irish Poetry', he scorned the 'anti-quarians' who kept alive the Revivalist spirit by writing about Irish myth and legend (D 70). Art for Beckett was timeless, the very opposite to politics and nationalism. He praises the paintings of Jack B. Yeats (brother of the poet and one of Beckett's heroes) for 'Strangeness so entire as even to withstand the stock assimilation to holy patrimony, national and other' (D 149). Beckett set out to resist assimilation to any cultural context or holy patrimony.

Nonetheless, he always chose to hold an Irish passport. When a journalist asked him if he was English, he replied, simply, 'Au contraire'. Evidently, he cannot be confined to simply one literary or national tradition. He is not exclusively anything – neither just an 'Irish' writer nor just a 'French' one, neither just a modernist nor just a postmodernist. 'The danger is in the neatness of identifications', begins Beckett's essay on Joyce's 'Work in Progress' (D 19). It is a warning well taken when trying to read his work, but it also applies to pigeon-holing him in any particular literary or intellectual tradition. Like any great writer, he is resistant to compartmentalisation. In considering Beckett's relationship with Ireland, we should make connections without making consolidations, applications rather than appropriations. Beckett is energised from many different national literatures – Irish, French, even German. One does not necessarily exclude the other. It is a crude and sclerotic opposition to pit the metropolitan against the national, as if a writer can belong only to one or the other. Joyce succeeded in merging both and so too does Beckett. Notwithstanding Beckett's resistance to 'local' substance and accident, the Irish vein in his work runs deep, even when it is not visible on the surface.

Not just his nationality, but also his particular class and caste within Irish society can be fruitfully brought to bear on his aesthetic and intellectual development. As I argued in Chapter 1, the political insulation of Beckett's middle-class, Protestant, suburban upbringing made it in some ways an easy move for him to scorn socially committed or national art, just as when he was in Germany in the thirties he could show impatience at the complaints of some of his fellow artists at Fascist persecution. It is as if not only politics, but social context as a whole is separable from artistic creativity which operates on a higher, trans-historical plane.

His political consciousness seems to have been transformed by the war and its aftermath, just as his prose voice lost its hauteur and sardonic tone. '*Molloy* and the others came to me the day I became aware of my own folly. Only then did I begin to write the things I feel.'[1] In his post-war career, though his work became ever less connected to a recognisable world, one could say, paradoxically, that it became more political, more shaped by exploitative power relations, edicts handed down from above, secrecy and inscrutability and descriptions of raw human torment. Beckett seems to have had a unusually acute sensitivity to the suffering of other sentient beings, including animals. Even in childhood he was traumatised by sights of cruelty, which would haunt him for years afterwards. It was just that in his younger years, and partly because of his insulated upbringing, this disposition never found an expression in political terms. His first motivation for joining the French Resistance seems to have been personal. He was appalled at the persecution of Jewish people, including some of his friends, by the Nazi forces occupying Paris. This may have been a key moment in his recognition that, even if the human suffering is inevitable, simply the result of being alive, then it was all the more intolerable that people should be tortured, abused or humiliated by other people. He began to develop, that is to say, a political sensibility. His horror of injustice and, in particular, torture manifested itself in later life in his opposition to French brutalities in Algeria, to the apartheid regime in South Africa (he refused to allow his plays to performed in segregated theatres) and to human rights abuses behind the Iron Curtain.

Nonetheless, there has been a strand of Beckett reception which sees him not just as apolitical, but as unique and autonomous, standing outside all available categories almost as if he is working in a vacuum. This is partly due to the force of Beckett's originality, his genius for mastering and making into his own every literary form in which he worked. The bare stages and stark images, the seeming investment in elemental and unmediated conditions of experience, reinforce the impression of a writer in quarantine from his historical moment. Yet for all his pre-war insistence on the universal and issueless relevance of art, for all the deracinated and rootless qualities of his own work, it is both undesirable and, happily, impossible for a writer to so wholly dislocate from his context to this extent. To quote the philosopher Schopenhauer on Dante: 'For whence did Dante get the material for his hell, if not from this actual world of ours?'[2] Beckett's work is notorious for its intense preoccupation with pessimism and human suffering, notwithstanding its bleak beauty and darkly acid comedy. Could anyone seriously hold that it is irrelevant or coincidental that Beckett lived through, indeed his life was almost concurrent with, the darkest and most brutalised century in recorded history? Two world wars, the horrors of Stalin, the Holocaust of Hitler, the disastrous Great Leap of Mao, brutal colonial wars in Africa and the protracted threat of atomic annihilation during the Cold War surely creep into a receptive mind at some level. They certainly generate an infecting atmosphere within the morale and outlook of Western culture as a whole, which could not but affect the creative imagination of an attuned artist. Beckett's adolescence in Ireland coincided with the Anglo-Irish War followed by the Irish Civil War. He visited Germany during the Fascist regime and, as already seen, partook in the struggle against Nazi power in Paris. These may not occur in the surface representations of Beckett's work, but the aftershocks they emitted through the values, beliefs and attitudes of the societies in which he lived and thought surely passed through and to some extent moulded his creative intelligence.

The devastations and despair of the twentieth century were felt in the other broadly pessimistic philosophical or literary movements, such as existentialism or the Literature of the Absurd, which took hold in Europe during the forties and fifties, and to which Beckett is sometimes (though not always appropriately) allied. Existentialism comes in many guises and, possibly more than any other philosophical movement, has a popular and simplified, even caricatured image. The term is generally used to refer to a philosophical movement associated with a number of post-war French thinkers, principally Jean-Paul Sartre and Albert Camus, which places the individual or the self at the centre of investigation and sees it as the basis for understanding the nature of human existence. The term derives in opposition to 'essentialism'. Existence, for Sartre, famously precedes essence, there is no blueprint for who we are or how we should behave, no authority from a God or any objective truth that validates our existence. The self is utterly alone. This primacy of the individual and of individual choice over any determinist systems of social or biological control leads to a strong emphasis on the concept of human freedom. Our freedom is inescapable, an intrinsic part of our loneliness and alienation. It is very tempting to deny it, to slough off the reality of our complete agency in an external role (like Watt in Mr Knott's house) or in some delusory system of purpose of belief (waiting for a Godot to arrive). But this is to be guilty of 'bad faith' and to fail to adopt a properly 'authentic' awareness of our freedom of choice.

There are certain similarities with some existentialist principles and Beckett's work – his play *Eleutheria* (the Greek for 'freedom'), in particular, bears some interesting parallels – but it is hard to be sure how much of these are just Beckett arriving at similar conclusions through a different route and how many occasions of actual influence. The obsessive interest in systems and determinism in many of Beckett's writings, the prevalent idea, as Hamm puts it in *Endgame*, that 'something is taking its course', kicks against the existentialist refusal of structure or control outside of human consciousness. It is not surprising that he told James Knowlson, in a conversation about existentialism, that he was more drawn intellectually to the deterministic notion that we are trapped by our genes, by our upbringing or by our social conditioning than to the existentialist idea of absolute freedom.[3]

There may be more affinity with another association of existentialism and Beckett's beliefs, namely the idea of 'absurdity', though here too caution is advised. Without any grounding, without any reason for our being in the world, a certain strand of existentialist thought concludes that life is absurd, disordered and meaningless. We are an accident of the universe, there is no plan or purpose for our lives and the really big question, which Albert Camus asks in *Le Mythe de Sisyphe* (*The Myth of Sisyphus*) (1942), is whether to commit suicide (significantly, a considerable temptation in *Waiting for Godot*). The category of 'Theatre of the Absurd' was coined by the critic Martin Esslin to indicate a group of playwrights who give artistic articulation to the belief in absurdity expounded by Camus, the sense that human existence is futile and without meaning. Other playwrights usually included in the designation include Eugène Ionesco, Jean Genet and Arthur Adamov. The absurdist outlook is generally reflected in the form as well as the content of the plays, which, in order to create nightmare moods, tend to reject logical construction, clear character identity or coherent relations between cause and effect.

Beckett himself, for telling reasons, explicitly renounced any association with the Theatre of the Absurd or more particularly with the premises upon which the critical grouping was based. For him this term was too 'judgemental', too self-assuredly pessimistic:

> I have never accepted the notion of a theatre of the absurd, a concept that implies a judgement of value. It's not even possible to talk about truth. That's part of the anguish.[4]

Beckett's resistance here is part of his move away from philosophy and rationality to a far more confused, epistemologically humble condition. He has renounced the self-assured pessimism of *Proust* for a bewildered, anguished view of the world, one that can only be expressed through artistic demonstration rather than 'existential' assertion:

> One cannot speak anymore of being, one must speak only of the mess. When Heidegger and Sartre speak of a contrast between being and existence, they may be right, I don't know, but their language is too philosophical for me.[5]

It is true that Beckett has not trained as a professional philosopher but since he has supped deeply across the philosophical tradition from the pre-Socratics onwards and, since his work, particularly his early work, is crammed with philosophical allusion, there is something slightly disingenuous about the disavowal. It is a sign, rather, of his post-war hostility to the language of ratiocination and philosophy, memorably lampooned in Lucky's 'think' in *Waiting for Godot*. Beckett's later hostility to philosophy is, like the reformed smoker, probably fuelled by his own early immersion in it.

Whatever the misgivings of Beckett's relationships with existentialism and post-war pessimism, however ill at ease he sits in this philosophical context, it is worth noting that the climate in which these pessimistic philosophies and outlooks thrived, where the idea of the absurd had taken root, was favourable for the reception of his work. If the post-war *Zeitgeist* had not favoured such expressions of absurdity, would *Waiting for Godot* have achieved its success?

Beckett was a tremendous innovator and experimenter in whatever form he deployed. This is one reason why he has been described as the 'last modernist'. Ezra Pound's famous imperative, 'make it new', is one of the rallying calls of the modernist movement. Modernism is a term applied retrospectively to the wide range of experimental and avant-garde trends in the literature and other arts of the early twentieth century, including Symbolism, Dadaism, Vorticism, Imagism, Expressionism, Futurism and others too numerous to include. It can be perilous identifying common traits amongst so many disparate artistic credos, but, across its various strands, modernism tends to share a heavy consciousness of the contemporary world precisely as 'modern', a sense that changed cultural, social and intellectual contexts require new literary and artistic forms. Nineteenth-century realism is regarded as calcified and inadequate to express the conditions of modernity. Beckett refers in *Proust* to 'the grotesque fallacy of a realist art – "the miserable statement of line and surface", and the penny-a-line vulgarity of a literature of notations' (P 76). Modernist writers tended to see themselves as an avant-garde, disengaged from bourgeois values, and disturbed their readers by adopting complex and difficult new forms and styles. In 'Recent Irish Poetry' Beckett divides poets amongst those who show awareness of 'the new thing that has happened', namely 'the rupture in the lines of communication', and those like the twilighters or antiquarians who are in 'flight from awareness' (D 71). Both the tone and the sentiment are characteristic of a modernist stance. This is not surprising, since a crucial phase of Beckett's artistic incubation occurred in Paris in the Joyce circle. The two novelists who most influenced Beckett were Proust and Joyce. Joyce's *Ulysses* is regarded as the foremost example of the modernist novel, with its exhaustive experimentation with perspective and literary styles, its mythic reach and its heavy allusiveness. *Finnegans Wake*, during the composition of which Beckett gave practical help to the visually impaired Joyce, was even more elusive and difficult. The twenty-three-year-old Beckett's essay defending the novel admires its fusion of form and content and declares, 'if you don't understand it, Ladies and Gentlemen, it is because you are too decadent to receive it' (D 26).

This essay was first published in *transition*, an avant-garde literary magazine subtitled 'An International Quarterly for Creative Experiment', which became an important platform for anti-bourgeois art and literature. Along with his essay on 'Work in Progress' Beckett also published his first short story, 'Assumption', in this issue.[6] There could hardly be a more avowedly modernist launchpad for a literary career. The fiction and poetry he went on to publish in the thirties continues to deploy many anti-realist procedures, often thwarting linearity and flaunting its own fictive qualities and, like much modernist literature, wears its learning somewhat on its sleeve.

Not much grows in the shade and there is no longer literary shadow in the twentieth century than that cast by Joyce. Many imitators and disciples withered in his influence. Beckett was aware of this danger (he remarked of his first novel, *Dream of Fair to Middling Women*, that it 'stinks of Joyce') and at first countered it in these early works through parody. As already seen in Chapter 1, he found a more permanent solution by moving in precisely the opposite direction, away from omniscience and omnipotence towards an art of impotence and ignorance, shedding the allusions and third-person know-ing, narrative voice for a much more inward and immersive first-person prose.

The impulse to shed also made itself felt in his drama, which from the start (if we except the large cast of *Eleutheria*) adopted a spare and unadorned stage setting. But it was not just props and cast who were dropped – Beckett abandoned the whole convention of playwriting, the idea that a play should have a beginning, a middle and an end, the notion that characters should be consistent and plausible, the presumption that action and plot were necessary to create dramatic energy. In the English-speaking world, modernist experi-ment and 'difficulty' had not impacted on the drama as much as in poetry or the novel, not least because theatre had additional commercial exigencies. There was a larger onus on theatres to conform to public taste and expect-ation, to provide a diverting evening of leisure. Popular theatre, before the arrival of cinema and television, tended to offer melodramas and light comedies. Even Beckett's fellow Old Portoran Oscar Wilde, though his layered and complex plays secrete subversive themes about the ambivalence of identity, chose the conventional form of the drawing-room comedy. Vaudeville and the music hall, with variety shows of singing, dancing and humorous sketches often involving comic pairings – forerunners of both Laurel and Hardy and Vladimir and Estragon – were common entertain-ments. The founders of a serious, literary European drama, offering social and psychological insight, were the Norwegian Henrik Ibsen (1828–1906) and the Russian Anton Chekhov (1860–1904). Ibsen was a key influence on George Bernard Shaw (1856–1950), a colossus of the British stage in the first half of the twentieth century.

Beckett was certainly not the first playwright to rupture realist conventions or to highlight the fictive nature of the theatre. As early as the twenties, Luigi Pirandello was writing plays that eschewed the comforts of illusion or the willing suspension of disbelief, with for instance supposed audience members walking onto stage and participating in the action, a technique Beckett would use in *Eleutheria*. The Marxist playwright Bertolt Brecht's (1898–1956) elaborately non-realist plays made a political point of undermining any identification between audience and character, seeking instead an alienation effect which would raise the historical consciousness and objectify capitalist reification. Brecht was one of the foremost playwrights of his era but his politics were surely too didactic and too explicitly political for Beckett. One could imagine his displeasure if Brecht had succeeded in his ambition before his death to write a counter-play to *Waiting for Godot* in which the relationship between Pozzo and Lucky would have been worked out in accordance with the Marxist view of history.[7]

Beckett's range of reading was prodigious, his saturation in European philosophy, literature, drama, art and music too vast for summary. He read widely in at least four languages, English, French, Italian and German. Any list of his literary influences would include Racine, Molière, Swift, Samuel Johnson (on whom, before his years of fame, he wrote an unfinished play called 'Human Wishes'), Goethe, Synge, Proust and Joyce. Special mention should perhaps be made of Dante Alighieri (1265–1321), the Italian author of *The Divine Comedy*, arguably the source of most abiding fascination for Beckett. The hero of *More Pricks than Kicks*, Belacqua Shuah, is named after an indolent character in Dante's *Purgatorio*. Throughout his work vivid images of suffering from Dante's masterpiece often resurface. Appropriately, Beckett's student copy of *The Divine Comedy* would be at his bedside as he died in December 1989.

He read a lot of philosophy in the 1930s, including the pre-Socratics, St Augustine, Descartes, the occasionalists, Bishop Berkeley (the inspiration for *Film*), Spinoza, Leibniz, Kant, Schopenhauer, Mauthner and Bergson. And his artistic interests and influences were emphatically not restricted to the written word. His passion for the Old Masters remained with him throughout his life and he was an admirer of many modern painters. His personal friends included Bram and Geer Van Velde, Henri Hayden and Avigdor Arikha, and he owned paintings by all these artists. At a time of penury in his early life, he once pushed himself into further hardship by buying a Jack B. Yeats painting. He was an accomplished pianist and a lover of the music of Schubert, Beethoven, Chopin and Mozart. The strongly visual qualities of his later drama, which sometimes seem closer to painting or sculpture than to traditional theatre, were in their turn greatly inspirational to many modern painters and visual artists. His passion for art and music is central to his elevation of form, shape and symmetry in his literary and dramatic practice.

Chapter 3

Plays

Waiting for Godot

The scene, and the action (or lack of it), are unmistakable: a bare country road with a mound and a tree, two elderly tramps wait for their appointment with a man called Godot, who never comes. This spare, nondescript setting for Beckett's first performed play has become one of the iconic images not just of modern drama but of the twentieth century itself. The meaning of the play is less certain. One of the first questions that spectators of the play often ask is who (or what) is Godot? Perhaps he represents 'God'? The boy who appears at the end of each act claims that Godot has a long white beard, like some pictorial representations of God in the West (or like a child's image of God) and that he keeps sheep and goats. (According to the Gospel, God will separate the righteous from the damned by putting the 'sheep' on his right side, 'goats' on his left (Matthew 25: 32–3).) After all, Godot gives Estragon and Vladimir a sense of direction and purpose in their lives (however misplaced), in a manner analogous to religious belief. Could the play, then, be an allegory for a post-theistic existence? Written in the shadow of the Second World War, God/Godot seems to have deserted a world mutilated by barbarism, mass destruction and genocide. His absence has left a hole which unavailing desire and expectation vainly try to fill.

But caution is required here. Beckett's work always resists singular explanation. Beckett's answer to the question 'Who is Godot?' was always, 'If I knew, I would have said so in the play.' When the eminent actor Ralph Richardson, a prospective Vladimir in the first London production, inquired of Beckett if

Godot was God, Beckett responded that had he meant God he would have said God and not Godot.[1] Godot's name resembles, but at the same time is more than, 'God'. Given that the play is replete with biblical allusion and deals with fundamental issues of time, desire, habit, suffering and so on, it is not too extravagant to recognise a religious element to the play, and to the figure of Godot, while still drawing back from a complete identification.

There might be a lesson here as to how we might read the play as a whole. *Waiting for Godot* is full of suggestion, but it is not reducible to exact allegorical correspondence. Beckett described it as 'striving all the time to avoid definition'.[2] The play will not be pinned down or located, a clear meaning will not arrive for us, just as Godot does not arrive for Vladimir and Estragon. They can be confused and uncertain about where they are, where they were and where they will be, and the audience, by extension, can feel bewildered by the elusive themes of a play which, while orbiting around philosophical and religious issues, tends to keep them at a distance, to keep us in a state of interpretative suspension.

To tie *Waiting for Godot* too closely to the religious metaphor might be to restrain its suggestive power. There are philosophical and psychological as well as theological dimensions to Godot's non-arrival. He can be seen to stand in for all striving, all hope, the tendency for us to live our lives geared towards some prospective attainment. Most human beings live in a constant state of yearning (low- or high-level) and fix onto some hope or desire for the future: the holiday just round the corner, the right job, the well-earned retirement. Once that hope is achieved or desire fulfilled, it moves on to some other object. As Beckett puts it in *Proust*,

> We are disappointed at the nullity of what we are pleased to call attainment. But what is attainment? The identification of the subject with the object of his desire? The subject has died – and perhaps many times – on the way.   (P 13–14)

According to the pessimistic philosophy advanced in Beckett's early essay (heavily influenced, as it is, by the nineteenth-century German philosopher Arthur Schopenhauer), the self is fragmented and distended through time and is better understood as a series of selves. Once one ambition or urge is fulfilled, desire shifts promiscuously on to another prospective attainment. Ultimately it cannot be fulfilled: 'whatever the object, our thirst for possession is, by definition, insatiable' (17). Life then becomes about a vain, future-orientated expectation of a Godot who does not arrive. We fill our days with routines and habits in expectation of this arrival, rarely stopping to confront the desperate situation in which we live – the scarcity and provisionality of fulfilment, the terrible destructiveness of time, the inevitability of death from the very moment of birth ('the grave-digger puts on the forceps' (90–1)).

At least three features of the play, however, redeem this bleak and pessimistic view of life. First, there is a fellow-feeling and kindness between Estragon and Vladimir. Second, the play is extremely funny, with that distinctly Beckettian comedy – dark, daring, intelligent and disturbing – that has the same roots as tragedy, rather than simply providing comic relief from it. As Nell remarks in Beckett's next play, *Endgame*, 'nothing is funnier than unhappiness' (20). Third, the writing and theatrical structure are meticulously poised and often beautifully crafted. It is frequently the case in Beckett's work that the form, which is always so scrupulous, precise and painstaking, has a symmetry and a serenity which brushes against the seemingly chaotic and miserable life conditions that are being described. *Waiting for Godot* does not have the quasi-musical shapes and patterns of Beckett's later minimalist 'dramaticules'. But the dialogue and the action here have a precision and a spare beauty that, one could argue, counters the ostensibly pessimistic subject matter. Without these finely honed techniques, Beckett could not have taken drama into the unexplored territory of boredom and stasis, while still maintaining theatrical energy. This is a play after which world drama would never be the same again. Many commentators would now hold it up as the most important play of the twentieth century. Deservedly or not, it is the single work for which Beckett is most well known and the work that transformed him, at forty-seven years of age, from a relatively obscure experimental novelist into a figure of global cultural importance.

The question of what or who Godot might be is only one of the perplexities in a play replete with meanings withheld and explanations denied. It is a play which can still confound students and theatre-goers, just as it did many of the initial audiences, who often responded with bewilderment and hostility. Why do the men seem incapable of leaving this spot? What separates the two acts? Why are there leaves on the tree in the second act but not the first? Why does Lucky allow himself to be so abused by Pozzo? What are we to make of the allusions to the crucifixion and to the Garden of Eden? It might be worth bearing in mind that the audience's lack of certainty is also shared by the two leads:

> ESTRAGON: We came here yesterday.
> VLADIMIR: Ah no, there you're mistaken.
> ESTRAGON: What did we do yesterday?
> VLADIMIR: What did we do yesterday?

ESTRAGON: Yes.

VLADIMIR: Why . . . (*Angrily*) Nothing is certain when you're
about. (14)

The desperate unreliability of memory is reinforced in Act II, as Estragon and
Vladimir once again falteringly try to figure out whether they were there the
day before or not. Estragon, who is less certain and less interested in the past
than Vladimir, can't recognise his boots in the middle of the stage. Vladimir
is discomfited by the leaves that have appeared on the tree. It is partly as an
antidote to this bewilderment that they embrace the one guiding principle of
which they can be sure: 'What are we doing here, *that* is the question. And we
are blessed in this, that we happen to know the answer. Yes, in this immense
confusion one thing alone is clear. We are waiting for Godot to come –' (80).

From the audience's point of view, one effect of the lack of definition, the
withholding of a clear meaning, is to shift the attention on to the dramatic
qualities of the play rather than the significance of its message, its function
rather than its meaning. It is clearly an innovatory and experimental play,
removed from the conventions of naturalist drama. The notion of plot is
fairly routed here. A clear relationship between cause and effect, the sequence
of exposition, complication and resolution, is thwarted, as we would expect
in a play which makes withheld knowledge not only its theme but also its
method. That the second act is so suggestive of a repetition of the first
(together with intimations that both 'days' might be part of an endless cycle)
complicates the relationship of cause and effect, or the progression from
beginning to middle to end, that audiences weaned on the well-made-play
would expect. And the tightly knitted plot, where all the strands of the play
are tied neatly into an intricate and satisfying pattern, is far more ragged here,
with jokes and stories left unfinished, information continually withheld and
events occurring with no seeming cause or connection. By whom and why
does Estragon get beaten every night? When did the two men make their
appointment to see Godot? Or is this just a figment of their unreliable
memory? Why does Godot beat one of the boys but not his brother? Why
was one of the thieves saved, but not the other? Why does Godot not come?
We too will wait in vain for definitive answers to these questions.

In order to make theatre of this condition, Beckett must rewrite the rule-
book, strive for a new grammar of the stage, more anti-dramatic than dramatic, which will resist exposition, climax and dénouement and incarnate
boredom, inaction and opacity. In order to understand his method, one could
point at the very first line of the play, 'Nothing to be done' (9). Action
presupposes a reasonably autonomous self and a world of intelligible causality,

and, since neither is available in Beckett's plays, there is little action on his stage. Estragon's famous description of the play in which he appears – 'Nothing happens, nobody comes, nobody goes, it's awful!' (41) – is wryly summed up by the critic Vivian Mercier's pithy quip that this is a play in which, 'nothing happens, twice', probably the most commonly quoted critical remark about *Waiting for Godot*.[3]

But on the other hand is 'waiting' itself not a sort of action? To be sure the notion of action is here extended into an area previously deemed ineffective in the theatre. Inertia, punctuated with inconsequential dialogue, sustains a large part of the play. But, against Mercier, it is clearly not the case that *nothing* happens here. Even apart from the arrival of Pozzo and Lucky, which brings a welcome injection of energy into both acts, a range of movement and activity takes place: playing with boots, exchanging hats, trousers falling down, characters running on and off. Moreover, the conversation and physical exchanges between the two leads constitutes a sort of dramatic activity. Surely interaction cannot be so wholly severed from action? Yes, there is much that is trivial and uneventful – mocking the gestures towards religious and philosophical profundity – but there is action in this play. Not just action, but a lot of rather vivid farce occurs on stage, pratfalls and antics that we might associate with the music hall or vaudeville (one of the acknowledged popular influences on which the play draws).

Realist drama hides its fictive, theatrical nature in its efforts to reproduce the appearance of the 'real' world. But *Waiting for Godot* is theatre which continually declares its own theatrical artifice. The idea of play and of play-acting operates within it on a number of levels. First, we have many self-conscious performances, the idea that the dialogue between Vladimir and Estragon is a kind of a 'game': 'Come on, Gogo, return the ball, can't you, once in a way?' (12). The performative quality is especially evident in Act II, when, to pass the time as usual, the pair 'play' at being Pozzo and Lucky. This metatheatrical element – the play's awareness of itself as a play – refuses the suspension of disbelief central to realism on the stage. If Vladimir and Estragon can pretend to be Pozzo and Lucky, then how can we be sure that Pozzo and Lucky are not just doing the same thing? Given that this *is* a play, we know of course that they are doing so – actors are playing all five parts and will do so again and again until the end of the run. There are several suggestions that the two acts are part of an ongoing cycle, and not just because of the many similarities between both days on which the acts supposedly take place. At the end of Act I, Vladimir remarks that the appearance of Pozzo and Lucky has changed, as if he and Estragon have met them before. At the end of Act II, he anticipates that they will be returning to the same spot tomorrow. So, in a sense, the repetition *in* the play, the suggestion that the activities are part of an ongoing cycle, reproduces the repetition *of* the play, the fact that the play is put on night after night.

Most people's lives involve a cycle or a routine of some sort, whether this is as prosaic as the working day or the rituals of getting up, eating and going to bed. Most of us develop habits or recurring patterns of behaviour that we follow rather unreflectively until some crisis or unusual event in life breaks through them. 'Habit', Vladimir declares, 'is a great deadener' (91). So the idea of repetition resonates with a certain aspect of day-to-day life at its most remorselessly mundane. However, at the same time it obviously reflects what actually happens in a play: actors turning up night after night to deliver lines that they have delivered before and will deliver again. In this way *Waiting for Godot* brings its own status as a piece of theatre into thematic alignment with a pessimistic view of life as repetition and habit. If conventional realist drama strives to mirror life, then this play, by contrast, shows how much life mirrors drama.

There are other metatheatrical techniques in the play subtly integrated into the action and texture of the language. So we do not have characters marching on stage from the auditorium (as we do, say, in Beckett's *Eleutheria*, the Pirandellesque play he wrote just before *Waiting for Godot*, unpublished during his lifetime and as yet unperformed), but we do have lots of activity within the play which self-reflexively borrows theatrical language. So, for instance, Vladimir runs off-stage in answer to one of the urgent calls of his defective bladder and the two actors playfully pretend to be fellow spectators of a performance:

> ESTRAGON: End of the corridor, on the left
> VLADIMIR: Keep my seat.
> (*Exit Vladimir*)   (35)

Throughout the play the characters make remarks, usually pejorative, about the way their exchanges are going: 'This is becoming really insignificant,' Vladimir disdainfully points out at one point (68). We also have more overt self-reflexive exchanges such as the following:

> VLADIMIR: Charming evening we're having.
> ESTRAGON: Unforgettable.
> VLADIMIR: And it's not over.
> ESTRAGON: Apparently not.
> VLADIMIR: It's only beginning.
> ESTRAGON: It's awful.
> VLADIMIR: Worse than the pantomime
> ESTRAGON: The circus.

VLADIMIR: The music-hall.
ESTRAGON: The circus. (34–5)

This exchange is a comment on the sort of play-acting that the two vagrants get up to in order to pass the time while waiting for Godot. But at the same time as it passes judgement on these exchanges, it also forms a part of them – it is just such a music hall exchange itself. Furthermore it humorously operates as a parody of the sort of snobbish conversation that might take place in the bar of the theatre during the interval. This brings the performance on stage, with all its inherent pretence, into alignment with the pretence and affectations of the world off-stage. So, again, the stage here is not passively seeking to reproduce 'real life' in the manner of naturalist drama. Rather it is demonstrating how the pretences and repetitions of drama are themselves reflections of life. So *Waiting for Godot* is a play that does something more radical than simply bringing reality into a performance – it is showing the performative, theatrical and repetitive aspects of what we call reality.

Often these metatheatrical aspects to the play take on the quality of parody, especially when aimed at the jaded theatrical traditions that are being overturned. So, for instance, Pozzo's attempt at an elegy for the setting sun seems like a send-up of portentously lyrical or poetic language:

> It is pale and luminous like any sky at this hour of the day. (*Pause.*) In these latitudes. (*Pause.*) When the weather is fine. (*Lyrical.*) An hour ago (*he looks at his watch, prosaic*) roughly (*Lyrical*) having poured fourth ever since (*he hesitates, prosaic*) say ten o'clock in the morning (*Lyrical*) tirelessly torrents of red and white light it begins to lose its effulgence, to grow pale (*gestures of the two hands lapsing by stages*) pale, ever a little paler, a little paler until (*dramatic pause, ample gesture of the two hands flung wide apart*) pppfff! finished! it comes to rest. (37–8)

The intertwining of the pretentiously lyrical and the mundanely prosaic, here reinforced by the shifting stage directions, comically deflates this elegy. As Pozzo will bitterly come to realise when he himself is devastated by the ravages of time, loss and degeneration cannot be sweetened by pat lyrical eloquence.

There is a sense in which any language which strives to be over-expressive, whether in the lyricism of Pozzo or the philosophising of Lucky, is derided. Lucky's 'think' is a parody of academic rhetoric and the blunt instrument of theological and philosophical inquiry:

> Given the existence as uttered forth in the public works of Puncher and Wattmann of a personal God quaquaquaqua with white beard

> quaquaquaqua outside time without extension who from the heights of
> divine apathia divine athambia divine aphasia . . .   (42–3)

Showy soliloquy and bluntly abstract philosophical ideas are ungainly expressive mechanisms for Beckett. The key Beckettian principle, which will lead to the ever greater diminution and 'purification' of his work as he gets older, is that expressive language is not to be trusted, that shape and silence are where artistic impact lies. Even as early as 1937, long before his post-war revelation, Beckett has registered his dissatisfaction with language, his desire to find expressiveness in the spaces in between words. In a famous letter to Axel Kaun, he speaks of his quest to tear holes in language: 'more and more my own language appears to me like a veil that must be torn apart in order to get at the things (or the Nothingness) behind it' (D 172). Not surprisingly, then, the most expressive moments in his plays often occur in the pauses and silences, indicating, at turns, repression, fear, anticipation or horrified inarticulacy. This pressing reality of the silence in *Waiting for Godot* is, as Beckett put it, 'pouring into this play like water into a sinking ship'.[4] Much of what Beckett has to say in his drama lies in what is omitted, when his characters cannot muster the words or the play-acting to forestall the encroaching silence, or the 'dead voices' that haunt Vladimir and Estragon when they stop speaking:

ESTRAGON:	In the meantime let us try and converse calmly, since we are incapable of keeping silent.
VLADIMIR:	You're right, we're inexhaustible.
ESTRAGON:	It's so we won't think.
VLADIMIR:	We have that excuse.
ESTRAGON:	It's so we won't hear.
VLADIMIR:	We have our reasons.
ESTRAGON:	All the dead voices.
VLADIMIR:	They make a noise like wings.
ESTRAGON:	Like leaves.
VLADIMIR:	Like sand.
ESTRAGON:	Like leaves.
	(*Silence.*)
VLADIMIR:	They all speak together.
ESTRAGON:	Each one to itself.
	(*Silence.*)
VLADIMIR:	Rather they whisper.
ESTRAGON:	They rustle.
VLADIMIR:	They murmur.
ESTRAGON:	They rustle.
	(*Silence.*)

[. . .]

VLADIMIR:	They make a noise like feathers.
ESTRAGON:	Like leaves.
VLADIMIR:	Like ashes.
ESTRAGON:	Like leaves.
	(*Long silence.*)
VLADIMIR:	Say something!
ESTRAGON:	I'm trying.
	(*Long silence.*)
VLADIMIR:	(*In anguish.*) Say anything at all!
ESTRAGON:	What do we do now?
VLADIMIR:	Wait for Godot.
ESTRAGON:	Ah!
	(*Silence.*) (62–3)

The economic rhythms of this passage and the careful combinations of repetition and variation combine with a soothing susurration to eke out a compelling dissonance between the language and the characters' guilty torment. Vladimir and Estragon are too close: they listen to the dead voices while we listen to the poetry. Hence Vladimir's desperate 'Say something!' after the long silence at the end of the exchange. The passage does not express their torment directly, but rather catches those dead voices elliptically, in the excruciating pauses.

Here as elsewhere the exchanges have an eerie, pre-ordained quality, reinforcing the point about the performative, repetitive, self-consciously theatrical dimension to the play. It is as if when Vladimir says something Estragon's reply has already been decided (which of course it has, since both speak from a memorised play script). Their exchanges are often constituted of one- or two-word utterances, carefully shaped into repetition and variation, giving them a poetic, estranging quality that unsettles the colloquial banality. Nonetheless, performance in a theatre renders the *unsaid* as present as the said, and, for all their spare beauty, these carefully pruned exchanges are scarcely enough to block out an encroaching and terrifying silence. This is why, presumably, Estragon and Vladimir are so desperate to keep the conversation alive, to block out the sound of the dead voices. Or perhaps to keep back the realisation that the silence brings: their conversations, like the waiting games they play, are a futile distraction from the destructiveness of time and the insatiability of desire. They are merely a 'habit' which protects them from the stricken awareness of their own abjection and solitude:

VLADIMIR:	All I know is that the hours are long, under these conditions, and constrain us to beguile them with proceedings

> which – how shall I say – which may at first sight seem
> reasonable, until they become a habit.   (80)

'Habit', once again, is a 'great deadener'. It deadens the suffering that too much awareness, too much reflection on the conditions of existence would bring. The daily routines, the various distractions of conversation and play-acting, are forms of self-protection.

There are clear differences between the two tramps. Estragon is preoccupied with physicality, the body, the earth. Not insignificantly, he tends to sit down far more than Vladimir. He is obsessed with his boots, whereas Vladimir often inspects his hat. Vladimir thinks, Estragon feels. At rehearsal, Beckett remarked of the pair: 'Estragon is on the ground; he belongs to the stone. Vladimir is light; he is oriented towards the sky.'[5] It is Vladimir who wonders about the two thieves crucified alongside 'Our Saviour', he who reflects on the nature of time at the end of the play. He who always answers Estragon's question about the purpose of their attendance at this spot:

> ESTRAGON: Let's go.
> VLADIMIR: We can't.
> ESTRAGON: Why not?
> VLADIMIR: We're waiting for Godot.
> ESTRAGON: Ah!   (78)

It is Vladimir who addresses the young boy at the end of each act, who experiences the philosophical insights. Many spectators record the impression that the two tramps feel like an old married couple, who bicker and quarrel – 'but for me . . . where would you be . . .?'; 'I'm tired telling you that' – and even threaten to leave each other. But underneath their irritations and impatience there is a close bond, and a recognition of their shared plight. 'We don't manage too badly, eh Didi, between the two of us?' (69). Vladimir is generally the protective one in the relationship. It was he who, they recollect, saved Estragon from drowning in the Rhône many years before, and he who, in one of the tenderest moments in the play, wraps his coat over the shoulders of the sleeping Estragon before walking up and down swinging his arms to keep warm. There are few enough consolations in a play about the futility of hope and desire, but these small moments of kindness, frail and unavailing though they may be, reveal shards of fellow-feeling and human decency that are at some level redemptive.

But if the play recognises moments of kindness brought on by adversity, it also highlights the brutality and domination that so often characterises human relations. Most obviously this occurs in Pozzo's treatment of Lucky, but even from Vladimir and Estragon the impulse to exploit emerges on occasion. When Pozzo reappears in Act II, Vladimir is intrigued to see his incapacity: 'You mean we have him at our mercy?' (78). The master–slave opposition between Pozzo and Lucky, the material exploitation of the latter by the former, is so elaborate that one is tempted to see it as a parody of the sort of social domination of which political radicals and reformers might complain. So exaggerated is Pozzo's maltreatment of Lucky, so hyperbolically and gratuitously brutal, that the niceties, formality and scrupulousness of his conversation with the two tramps seems comically anomalous. For all the refinement he shows to them – and in contrast to the utter inhumanity he shows to the hapless slave – he is aware of the difference in his own social rank and that of the two tramps: 'Yes, gentlemen, I cannot go for long without the society of my likes (*he puts on his glasses and looks at the two likes*) even when the likeness is an imperfect one' (21). The two vagrants also recognise social superiority when they see it. Pozzo is addressed as 'Sir', while Lucky only merits the less deferential 'Mister'. Such locutions as 'Oh I say!' or 'My good man' identify Pozzo as well-to-do English or, possibly, Anglo-Irish. Another facet of the power dynamic worthy of note here is that Lucky, while clearly standing in as an oppressed servant or slave, may also be the artist and intellectual figure. In the relationship of Pozzo and Lucky can be discerned a shadow of class relations between the land-owners or the wealthy and those that provide them with intellectual and aesthetic diversions: 'But for him all my thoughts, all my feelings, would have been of common things (*Pause. With extraordinary vehemence.*) Professional worries! (*Calmer*) Beauty, grace, truth of the first water, I knew they were all beyond me. So I took a knook.'[6] (33)

Pozzo remarks at one point that he could have been in Lucky's shoes, and vice versa, 'If chance had not willed otherwise' (31). It is a telling use of this cliché. How can chance 'will' something? Of its nature, chance is will-less, and inanimate, outside the operations of even a blind determinism. If something happens by accident or chance, then an act of will has nothing to do with it. But *Waiting for Godot* is a play which, from the beginning, seeks to probe the 'why' of suffering. Or, perhaps more accurately, seeks to dramatise the condition of not knowing the answer to this question. It begins, after all, by asking why one of the thieves was saved but not the other. On what basis was the selection made? At the end of Act I, we discover that Godot beats one of the boys but not his brother, but for what reason? The boy does not know. The refrain within Lucky's speech, a parody of academic or philosophical attempts to understand the source of human suffering, is that human beings suffer 'for reasons unknown'. Here is another echo of the non-arrival of Godot. Vladimir does not receive an answer to his initial questions about the crucifixion. The mystery remains unsolved.

It is not enough simply to declare that Beckett's characters are 'innocent' sufferers. The problem is rather that their crime, the source of their guilt, is elusive. Punishment and damnation are dished out for seemingly inscrutable reasons. In Western culture the ultimate source of guilt, the primal transgression, is Original Sin. This is the stain with which, in the Judeo-Christian tradition, each person is born. *Waiting for Godot*, as we have seen, playfully alludes to this Edenic source but simultaneously deflates it. Early in the play, the pair consider what it is they should repent:

> VLADIMIR: Suppose we repented.
> ESTRAGON: Repented what?
> VLADIMIR: Oh . . . (*He reflects.*) We wouldn't have to go into the details.
> ESTRAGON: Our being born?
> (*Vladimir breaks into hearty laugh which he immediately stifles, his hand pressed to his pubis, his face contorted.*)   (11)

Years before, in *Proust*, Beckett has made another allusion to the sin of birth as part of a definition of tragedy:

> Tragedy is not concerned with human justice. Tragedy is the statement of an expiation, but not the miserable expiation of a codified breach of local arrangement, organized by the knaves for the fools. The tragic figure represents the expiation of the original sin, of the original and eternal sin . . . of having been born.   (67)

This excerpt is full of philosophical confidence to the point of pomposity: true tragedy is original and eternal and not at all concerned with 'local' issues such as justice or history. This disdain for politically motivated art in Beckett's early critical work would seem to strengthen the hand of those commentators who read *Waiting for Godot* as about a universal human condition. However, there are important differences between the notion of birth as sin in *Proust* and its recurrence in *Waiting for Godot*. In the later instance the assertion that original sin ought to be 'expiated' (how the expiation is effected is not explained in *Proust*, though the implication is that it has something to do with the catharsis of tragedy) has become a joke. The grandiosity of the aspiration is immediately undercut first by Vladimir's guffaw and then by his attempt, prompted by his painful urinary complaint, to stifle it. Once again the 'big idea', that might give us an interpretative hook on the play, is punctured as soon as uttered.

There is little uncertainty about the tone of *Proust* which, as the disdain for the merely 'local' above attests, assumes a universal validity for its pessimistic pronouncements. 'Life' itself, marred as it is by destructive time and insatiable desire, is about boredom, habit and suffering. Blaming the debased condition of humanity on any political or social arrangements would be equivalent, to borrow a phrase of Vladimir's, to blaming on the boots the faults of the feet. From the earliest critical reception of *Waiting for Godot*, many commentators claimed that it had something fundamental to say about what it means to be human. In other words, the play does not simply have to do with particular people at a particular moment in history – it says something about the 'human condition' as a whole, outside history or politics, or any particular social situation.

The seeming withdrawal of *Waiting for Godot* from a world of specifics gives succour to this ahistorical view. The play is so bare and shorn of recognisable geographical reference that one might be tempted to read this as a sort of an archetypal space that can stand in for everywhere or anytime. The sparseness of the setting and the simplicity of the narrative suggest the play might be dealing with elemental truths. Admittedly there are a few scant references to particular places – to the Eiffel Tower, or to the River Rhône – which betray the original French in which the play was written. Lucky's reference to the 'skull in Connemara' gestures towards Beckett's Irish roots (though this is 'Normandie' in the original French version). Similarly Estragon asks Pozzo for ten francs. But at the same time there is a careful rootlessness in the staging and presentation. If Estragon's name has a French quality (it means tarragon), Vladimir's sounds more Russian. Pozzo's name sounds like a clown's and Lucky's like a household pet. In terms of their dialect, the two tramps speak English with an Irish cadence. So the national cues come from the various different parts of Europe with which Beckett was familiar. It leaves a plurality of sourcing that encourages the notion that this is everyplace. Vladimir ponders on Pozzo's call for assistance when he is prostrate in Act II: 'To all mankind they were addressed, those cries for help still ringing in our ears! But at this place, at this moment of time, all mankind is us, whether we like it or not' (79). A little later, Estragon remarks of Pozzo, 'He's all humanity' (83), just after the latter has answered to both the names Abel and Cain. We might remember that in the first act, Estragon has claimed his name is 'Adam', and of course one of the echoes of the lone tree on-stage is to the Garden of Eden. This association with the mythic origin of humankind allows the play to resonate, once more, with the elemental, the original and ultimately the universal. The answer, then, as to the representative status of the characters on stage is given by Estragon:

VLADIMIR: We have kept our appointment, and that's an end to that.
We are not saints, but we have kept our appointment. How
many people can boast as much?
ESTRAGON: Billions.   (80)

Lines like this are further encouragement to read the play as a sort of an
allegory of the human condition.

'The key word in my plays', Beckett told Tom Driver, 'is "perhaps".'[7] It is
paradoxical that a play with such an investment in the withholding of
certainty, in the processes of confusion and bewilderment, would make such
grandiose claims as to how things are. But, as ever, if this universal reading is
suggested, it is like the idea of Godot as God, only one of many interpretative
possibilities, all of which contribute to the overall aesthetic effect. The Edenic
allusion is often so flagrant here that it teeters into irony, undoing through
comic exaggeration any symbolic meaning it might hold. Moreover, how can
we trust Estragon? His assertion that 'billions' keep their appointment is
contradicted by his ignorance in almost all other facets. He cannot even
remember what happened the previous day, so why should we take uncritic-
ally his assertions of catholicity? He is less reflective and intellectual than
Vladimir and is mostly motivated by his next carrot or chicken bone.
Vladimir thinks about the Bible, whereas Gogo simply admires the illustrations of the Holy Land. It is telling that the references to Eden come from the
unreflective Gogo, rather than the cerebral and contemplative Vladimir.
From this source, the allusions to the mythic origins of humanity are no
sooner uttered than ridiculed.

The play is not translatable to a series of philosophical formulae nor,
simply, to a pessimistic view of the human condition. Just as Beckett was
uncomfortable with the label of 'Theatre of the Absurd', he disowned the idea
that he had a systematically negative view of life, or any sort of synoptic
overview from which judgement could be made:

> If pessimism is a judgement to the effect that ill outweighs good, then
> I can't be taxed with same, having no desire or competence to judge.
> I happen simply to have come across more of the one than the other.[8]

There is too much uncertainty in his work, too much doubt and bewilderment, for clear interpretations to provide pat certainty. This is a play in which
Godot does not arrive. Beckett renounced the abstract philosophical pronouncements of his younger self and, as we see from Lucky's 'think', came to
regard academic philosophy and theology with scepticism. One suspects that
Beckett was frustrated that the passages on time and habit in the play have

been continually used as interpretative hooks. He felt, significantly, that 'the early success of *Waiting for Godot* was based on a fundamental misunderstanding, critics and public alike insisted on interpreting in allegorical or symbolic terms a play which was striving all the time to avoid definition'.[9] *Waiting for Godot* is all about this avoidance of definition. Like Vladimir and Estragon, the audience and critics of the play are attendant on a meeting that is continually deferred.

Endgame

Endgame is set in a world even more unfamiliar than that of *Waiting for Godot*. All outside, if we are to believe the testimony of Clov and his telescope, is grey, deserted and lifeless. The characters have memories of a world similar to our own, but the one they live in is depleted and belated. Their memories are more attuned than the characters in *Waiting for Godot*, so their awareness of current dereliction is all the more of a torment. Physical debility is clearly a motif in the earlier play but in this world of the amputated, the paralytic and the blind, the sense of decrepitude and entrapment is far more oppressive. Outside, all is 'corpsed'. This desolate landscape resembles a post-apocalyptic scene, prompting some commentators to speculate on whether some of the anxieties of the Cold War, with the threat of nuclear extinction, can be felt in this play. The reason for why the world is at this point of expiration, why all outside is grey and flat and lifeless, is not given. Nor is the behaviour of the characters explained. Why does Clov do Hamm's bidding when he resents it so much? Why are Hamm's parents, the legless Nagg and Nell, confined to ashbins? What is the relationship of Hamm's chronicle to the play? Does it, as many have suggested, relate to the arrival of Clov in the house? At a production in the Riverside Studio in Hammersmith in 1980, directed by Beckett, Rick Cluchey, playing Hamm at the time, asked Beckett directly if the little boy in the story is actually the young Clov. 'Don't know if it's the story of the young Clov or not,' was Beckett's characteristic response. 'Simply don't know.'[10]

Spectators on the look-out for a meaning in the play will encounter the following metatheatrical snub: 'HAMM: We're not beginning to . . . to . . . mean something? CLOV: Mean something! You and I, mean something! (*Brief laugh.*) Ah that's a good one!' (27). If everything is coming to an end, if all is run down and exhausted, this does not just apply to painkillers and bicycles but to the less tangible qualities of meaning and clarity. The stage directions tell us that there is a picture facing the wall in the room where the action takes place, a metaphor perhaps for the withheld information throughout the play. Unlike the conventional or well-made play, we are not given the 'full picture' – not even at the end. Rather, we have to make do with the vague refrain: 'Something is taking its course.' What is this 'something', apart, obviously, from the already written play which is unfolding before our eyes? How do those aspects of *Endgame* which we might consider 'bewildering' or 'bizarre' actually function aesthetically or dramatically? How might we begin to 'read' or interpret them?

Endgame resists critical decoding or philosophical explanation to an even greater degree than *Waiting for Godot*. This resistance is part of its aesthetic and theatrical effect. *Waiting for Godot* also withholds certainty, as we saw, but there are reflections on time, habit, desire and so onto which a critic can gain a precarious grip. *Endgame* poses the sheerer challenge. It is as if, frustrated by the philosophical interpretations of *Waiting for Godot*, a 'play struggling at all times to avoid definition', Beckett has produced a new play immune to explanation in 'allegorical or symbolic terms'. However, if *Endgame* bypasses neat, rational explanation, this is not to say that it does not communicate in a powerful and affecting way. The German philosopher and critic T. W. Adorno, in possibly the most famous essay on this play, can praise it for putting 'drama in opposition to ontology', for dramatising an incoherent situation, untranslatable into the language of rationality and conceptuality: 'Understanding *Endgame* can only be understanding why it cannot be understood, concretely reconstructing the coherent meaning of its incoherence.'[11] Rather than simply asserting a lack of 'meaning', the play actually demonstrates it. This is why Adorno held that the play was so much more powerful that the existentialist philosophy with which Beckett was sometimes associated. In abstract philosophy, what we understand only occurs at the level of complexity and ideas. *Endgame* claws at deeper and darker levels of experience and intuition.

This is not simply to say that the play must be experienced, but cannot be interpreted or analysed. It does suggest that critical circumspection be maintained, a wariness of hidden meanings that unlock the play. Beckett, as already seen, refused to offer exegesis of any kind on *Endgame*, insisting instead on the 'extreme simplicity of dramatic situation and issue' (D 109). Sometimes, however, the 'simplicity' can be as elusive as complex and erudite pronouncements. Both thwart the expectations of familiarity. So, notwithstanding the dangers of 'headaches among the overtones', it might be helpful to clarify what determinate remarks we can make on *Endgame*, in what areas of human experience it is located. At its most obvious, it would, like *Waiting for Godot*, appear to take dramatic energy from particular human relationships.

However, the fellow-feeling that was evident in the earlier play, the tenderness between the two leads, is here harder to find. If it is anywhere, it is in the relationship between Nagg and Nell. For all Nagg's unseemly appetites – 'The old folks at home! No decency left! Guzzle, guzzle, that's all they think of' (15) – his relationship with Nell approaches intimacy more than any of the others. They speak tenderly to each other and Nagg keeps some of his biscuit to share with Nell, though she becomes lost in her own reveries about their time on Lake Como. Nagg could be an old Estragon, as concerned for his 'pap' and sugar plums as the other for his carrot and chicken bones, while Nell, more pessimistic, more cerebral and with a better memory than her husband, could be like Vladimir: 'Why this farce, day after day?' (18). The relationship between Hamm and Clov, by contrast, seems comparable to that between Pozzo and Lucky. Hamm shares much with Pozzo: his attention-seeking bombast, his capacity for cruelty, his vulnerability and need for reassurance, his sham lyricism. Clov, though surly at times, is a great deal more vocal than Lucky in expressing his disgust with his role in the world, but also seems to be in some sort of bondage to Hamm. It is a master–slave relationship based on mutual need but also entrapment: Clov, in answer to Hamm's statement 'I thought I told you to be off', replies 'I'm trying. (*He goes to door, halts.*) Ever since I was whelped' (17–18). Clov is irritated and tormented by Hamm (Clov is close to *clou*, the French for 'nail', Hamm close to 'hammer'), but at the same time he is capable of tending to him. When Clov pretends the dog is standing up for Hamm, it is almost as if he is a parent and Hamm a child that he seeks to placate.

For all the antagonism between Hamm and Clov, for all the difference in their role and character, they have one thing in common. They both suffer. Amongst the earliest lines of both, they reflect on their torment: 'CLOV: I can't be punished any more'; 'HAMM: Can there be misery – (*he yawns*) – loftier than mine?' (12). The yawn here, implying the bored or the jaded, contradicts the aspirations to grandeur of the word 'loftier'. It is the first sign of a careful blending of the inflated and the deflated, the turgid and the trivial. Similarly the action of the play is at once geared towards some quasi-climactic, long-awaited ending while at the same time dwelling on the dreary routines of day-to-day life. The anticipation in this play, which counters the boredom and inanity of the stage action, is not towards the Utopian, endlessly deferred arrival of a saviour but, more bleakly, towards the relief of a finish or conclusion. Like in *Waiting for Godot*, there is ambivalence or conflict here between 'time' as the source of decay and depletion and 'time' as a source of repetition and entrapment. That is time as bringing change and loss and time as simply cyclical, the routine that the characters in the play go through, which also makes a metatheatrical gesture towards the repetition of the play night after night until the end of the run. There is atrophy and loss here combined with stasis and inertia. For all the promises of ending, and for all the evident physical decay, Hamm ends up with the handkerchief over his face the same way he started (the last word in the play is 'remain') and Clov seems unable to leave the stage.

This ambivalent representation of time runs alongside the ambivalent attitude to loss and ending. We are told there are no more bicycles, no more lamp-oil, no more 'pap' or sugar plums or Turkish Delight for Nagg, no more painkiller for Hamm. There is much nostalgia in the play. To a far more intense degree than in *Waiting for Godot*, the characters are aware of what they have already lost, just as Nagg and Nell reminisce about their amorous youth and Hamm considers 'all those I might have helped'. Devastation and decay hence come to seem an exacerbation of their suffering, they yearn for the past when the world offered possibility and experience. 'Ah yesterday!' Nell elegiacally sighs. Of course, the glaze of nostalgia that coats these reminiscences borders on the hyperbolic and farcical. This suggests that, as ever in Beckett, voluntary memory is inherently distortive, deriving more from present needs than the actual experiences of the past. Nonetheless, whether real or imagined, the awareness of a loss, of a fall of some kind, is poignantly counterpointed with the devastated present, giving the play a more tragic quality than *Waiting for Godot*. It is, however, a very belated and depleted sort of a tragedy, in which we join the action after the loss has taken place and in which the sense of pathos is frequently undercut by farce and, more importantly, by inversions of the value-system which a sense of tragedy requires. Together with the nostalgia for the lost world, there is satisfaction that all is falling apart, and the whole sorry business of life is coming to an end. It causes pain to lose these things, just as the physical decay which Hamm predicts for Clov – when he will lose his sight and become as debilitated as Hamm himself – is a dreadful prospect. But at the same time, just as both Hamm and Clov yearn to finish, depletion and atrophy are welcomed. They signal the end and hence are a blessed relief. 'There are so many terrible things' laments Clov. 'No. No. There are not so many now' is Hamm's reassuring answer (33). Even though there is a poignancy and pain in there being so little left, there is still an urge to see the protracted ending continue. This world is so bad that its end is to be welcomed. Hence Hamm's repeated use of the word 'good' at the end of the play when it seems that Clov has gone (he has not) and he is left alone and helpless.

One area for which all the talk of 'finishing' certainly seems relevant is the metatheatrical elements of the play, the knowing hints to the fact that it *is* a play. At certain points these can be quite explicit, as with Clov's ironic description of the audience. He turns his telescope onto the auditorium and declares, 'I see . . . a multitude . . . in transports . . . of joy. (*Pause.*) That's what I call a magnifier' (25). These metatheatrical elements are even more histrionic than in *Waiting for Godot*, not least because they often come from the showy and performative Hamm. Like Estragon and Vladimir, Hamm and Clov sometimes pass judgements on their dialogue – 'This is slow work' or 'We're getting on' – but there are also more general allusions to theatrical language. So, for instance, when Clov threatens to leave and asks Hamm what reason there is for him to stay, Hamm answers 'The dialogue' (39). More explicit still is Hamm's angry rebuke to Clov for answering his 'aside', and hence not respecting the theatrical convention of asides and soliloquies whereby the other characters on stage pretend not to hear them: 'An aside, ape! Did you never hear an aside before? (*Pause.*) I'm warming up for my last soliloquy' (49).

On this level, all the talk about 'finishing' or 'ending' also refers to the roles they are playing. The fact that they want to end so much reinforces a familiar Beckettian theme where speech and play-acting become a sort of torture. On the one hand it keeps characters distracted and hence momentarily protected (think how Hamm loves to tell his story); on the other, the whole sorry business – the pretence, the 'entrapment' (in the sense of having to go through pre-ordained roles) and the repetition intrinsic to the play-acting – is conflated with existential tedium and angst more generally: 'Why this farce, day after day?' as both Nell and Clov remark. Again, as with *Waiting for Godot*, the subtle metatheatrical elements in *Endgame* do not only highlight theatre as theatre. At the same time they demonstrate the performative, repetitive and theatrical aspects of everyday life.

Another metatheatrical technique in *Endgame* is the parody of inflated theatrical language. The shards of pessimistic soliloquy that make it to the surface in *Waiting for Godot* never get beyond the mordant parody of Hamm's struggle for grandiloquence in *Endgame*. For all his aspirations to lofty misery, Hamm is a tragic hero depleted of lyricism, just as his name is an amputated version of Hamlet, the most famous tragic hero of all. Like the painkillers and everything else in this play, poetic language is fast disappearing. All that is left is his empty oratory and half-baked recitals. There is plenty of striving for the magisterial touch, especially in Hamm's attempt to tell his chronicle to his unwilling audience, but not much significance behind the portentousness:

> A little poetry. (*Pause.*) You prayed – (*Pause. He corrects himself.*) You
> CRIED for night; it comes – (*Pause. He corrects himself.*) It FALLS: now

cry in darkness. (*He repeats, chanting.*) You cried for night; it falls: now
cry in darkness. (*Pause.*) Nicely put, that. (*Pause.*)   (52)

Hamm is here the 'ham' actor, over-stretching his part and imbuing his tired
lines with a ponderous significance they do not merit. Bombastic language is
immediately deflated by the corporeal, the gross or the everyday: 'My anger
subsides, I'd like to pee' (22). Literary eloquence or grandeur, like natural
beauty, is no longer available in this world. Hamm's turgid attempts to
retrieve it simply serve to highlight the absence. His performance, however,
also emphasises the contingency and fragility of his own dominance over the
others, including the man in his chronicle who comes to him for help. Often
when Beckett is displaying exploitative power relations (Pozzo and Lucky is
another example) they become denaturalised through an intensification of
their performative element. Social roles and political hierarchies loosen when
they are shown to be a matter of 'play' or performance rather than a question
of naturally ordained and inescapable identity. Pozzo might have been in
Lucky's shoes, as he himself recognises, if chance had not willed otherwise.

The loftiness to which Hamm aspires makes the literary tradition seem
jaded and derivative. This might account for some of the intertextual allusion
in the play, especially to Shakespeare. 'My kingdom for a nightman!' (22)
clearly alludes to the famous plea in Shakespeare's *Richard III*, 'my kingdom
for a horse' (V, iv, 7). Clov's violent rebuke to Hamm, 'I use the words you
taught me. If they don't mean anything any more, teach me others. Or let me
be silent' (32), echoes that of Caliban to Prospero in Shakespeare's *The
Tempest*, 'You taught me language and my profit on't/Is, I know how to
curse: The red plague rid you/For learning language!' (I, ii, 365–7). Hamm's
'Our revels now are ended' (39) directly quotes Prospero in the same play (IV,
i, 148). Given Hamm's failure to achieve eloquence and the general refusal of
both thematic clarity and philosophical profundity in the play, the allusions
to Shakespeare just highlight an absence. When King Lear is stripped and
exposed during the storm on the heath, in a moment of elemental and
unrelenting extremity sometimes regarded as quasi-Beckettian, he can at least
rail against providence with expressiveness and insight. There is no such
facility in *Endgame*, so the Shakespearean quotations floating in this text are
like the flotsam and jetsam of a devastated literary tradition. They highlight
another loss.

Prospero in *The Tempest* is able to control the events on his island, up until
the loss of his magic powers at the end of the play. In *Endgame* the power of
human agency, far from magical, is severely circumscribed, and a general
sense of entrapment prevails. This is shown perhaps most obviously in the

physical disabilities of all four of the characters, but is no less implied by the general sense of determinism that pervades the play. In other words, the characters are not only trapped in something spatial – not even the relatively mobile Clov seems able to leave – but also in something temporal. 'Something is taking its course', as already noted, is the key refrain. There is a mechanical, clockwork feel to the movements on stage, a preoccupation with precision and pattern evinced, for instance in Hamm's obsession about finding the dead centre of the room. This is one of the ways in which the allusion to the chess game in the title operates. The action seems leached of human will, the characters here are chess-pieces being moved by forces outside their control.

> CLOV: Do this, do that, and I do it. I never refuse. Why?
> HAMM: You're not able to.
> CLOV: Soon I won't do it any more.
> HAMM: You won't be able to any more.   (31–2)

Human agency is ebbing into deterministic pattern. That the characters' actions are pre-ordained alludes most obviously to the theatrical fact that this is a play and hence based on a pre-written script. But it also perhaps derives from a more thematic and even philosophical approach to determinism. Beckett admitted that he finds deterministic accounts of life more convincing that the non-deterministic. His recognition that there are structures controlling human behaviour, limiting our freedom, places him in a different camp to the existentialists. He agreed enthusiastically with his biographer James Knowlson's objections to the existentialist emphasis on untrammelled human freedom, saying that he found 'the actual limitations on man's freedom of action (his genes, his upbringing, his social circumstances) far more compelling than the theoretical freedom on which Sartre had laid so much stress'.[12] Whether we are the product of nature (genes, biological determinism) or nurture (social conditioning, upbringing, ideology), Beckett is more drawn to the idea that human action is caught in delimiting systems and structures than that we have significant control over our behaviour. Such a view is evinced in the mechanical, coldly deterministic qualities of *Endgame*.

It might also help explain the attitude to 'nature' in this play. The comforts of natural beauty are thin in *Waiting for Godot*, occurring mostly in memories of earlier lives. But at least some leaves appeared on the tree in the second act. Hamm loves to dream about Nature; he often yearns for a pastoral alternative to the deserted greyness in which he lives. Sometimes his evocation of natural beauty is vivid and compelling. His is the Romantic idea in which Nature is a 'mother', a guarantor of authenticity and comfort. If he could fall asleep, he would 'go into the woods. My eyes would see . . . the sky, the earth. I'd run, run, they wouldn't catch me. (*Pause.*) Nature!' (19). The only woods left now are in Hamm's dreams. Whereas the dustbins of Nagg and Nell used to be lined with sawdust, now they have to rely on sand. But Hamm hopes that Nature endures elsewhere. 'Did you ever think of one thing?' he asks Clov. 'That here we're down in a hole. (*Pause.*) But beyond the hills? Eh? Perhaps it's still green. Eh? (*Pause.*) Flora! Pomona! (*Ecstatically.*) Ceres! (*Pause.*) Perhaps you won't need to go very far' (30). Nature's bounty delights Hamm, its absence (for all his yearning for an end) is part of his torment.

But if the products of Nature have gone, its *processes* endure. And they are part of the deterministic, entropic world in which the characters are trapped:

> HAMM: Nature has forgotten us.
> CLOV: There's no more nature.
> HAMM: No more nature! You exaggerate.
> CLOV: In the vicinity.
> HAMM: But we breathe, we change! We lose our hair, our teeth! Our bloom! Our ideals!
> CLOV: Then she hasn't forgotten us.
> HAMM: But you say there is none.
> CLOV: (*sadly*) No one that ever lived ever thought so crooked as we.   (16)

The pastoral solace of Nature has gone, but the blind destruction of natural change and decay has not. It is the worst of both worlds, the natural and the 'post'-natural. Clov's attempts at sprouting seeds end in failure, an emblem, perhaps, of the ineffectuality of human control over the natural world. Nature is random and blind, a source of constant struggle with no clear purpose or end, determinism without teleology, just as Darwin conceived of natural selection as struggle without a goal. This is why the prospect of evolution starting all over again is so galling. First, a flea or a crablouse appears in Clov's trousers. Hamm declares, 'But humanity might start from there all over again! Catch him, for the love of God!' (27). He strives to kill it with insecticide, but realises that it may simply be 'laying doggo'. Later, a rat appears in the kitchen, which escapes Clov's efforts to exterminate it. And finally, near the end, Clov sees a boy through his telescope, 'a potential procreator' (50). Clov has seen evolution progressing from flea to rat to boy. It is precisely as Hamm feared.

A world in which any trace of new life, including that of a young child, is to be immediately extinguished is not one which embraces a readily recognisable ethics. In *Endgame* the processes of negation are such that conventional values are overthrown. The supreme act of transgression is reproduction: 'Accursed progenitor!' Hamm shouts at his father (15). This is certainly a play about 'loss', but if loss is have to any significance it must concern something that has been valued and prized. The loss of refuse, or something regarded as disposable anyway, will not glean any recognition of significance, let alone achieve tragic grandeur. In *Endgame*, parents are kept in rubbish bins and the death of a mother is scarcely due a mention. It is as if 'value' itself, along with all the more tangible materials like painkillers and sugar plums, is in the process of running out. There are certainly layers of parody and black comedy in the depiction of Hamm's attitude to his parents (as indeed there is in his horror at the prospect of evolution starting all over again). But there is also a strongly subversive and shocking refusal of the values of life, the family, 'progress' and so on. Traditional bourgeois domestic drama fetishises and celebrates family relationships. Even if these relationships are destroyed or the family ends up grieving, they are a norm against which the tragic action makes sense. When that value itself is lost alongside everything else, as is the case in *Endgame*, the terminal sense of negation and obliteration takes us to a realm beyond or beneath tragedy. If the conventional tragic idiom to which this play aspires ('misery loftier than mine') articulates the values of tragic loss, this play moves to a more radical depletion in articulating the loss of tragic value.

Radio plays: *All That Fall* and *Embers*

We should be grateful to the BBC. Without the solicitations of the Third Programme, Samuel Beckett might never have explored the radio medium. The first of his radio plays, *All That Fall*, was broadcast on 13 January 1957. It was his first published play in English. Regarded almost immediately as a classic of the radio genre, it was repeated several times that year. More plays for the radio soon followed. *Embers* was broadcast on 24 June 1959; *Words and Music* on 13 November 1962. *Cascando* was written in French and broadcast by RTF in Paris on 13 October 1963. Its English version was produced by the BBC and broadcast on 6 October 1964.

These four pieces constitute Beckett's major works for radio. The only other piece to have been broadcast was *Rough for Radio*, an aptly named fragment aired on 13 April 1976. The flirtation with the airwaves appears to have been a way out of a logjam for Beckett. Following the exhaustive and exhausting experience of writing the trilogy the *Textes pour rien* (*Texts for Nothing*), as the title indicates, could not get him out of 'the attitude of disintegration'. Plays were still possible 'mais toujours dans la même direction [always in the same direction]'.[13] Experimentation in a fresh medium rejuvenated his creative powers. The new possibilities offered by radio profoundly affected his later work, the use of a tape recorder in *Krapp's Last Tape* being only the most obvious example. However, his radio plays are important accomplishments in their own right and, crucially, illustrate Beckett's mastery of whatever medium he exploited. Just as he had taken stagecraft back to its elementals, broadening and reinvigorating the possibilities of live theatre, so with the radio Beckett stretches and tests the form, exploiting the absence of a visual dimension and deploying the ethereality of the medium to create a tension between aural presence and physical absence.

The actual substance is entirely auditory, so there is a directly mediated link between the voice of the character and the ear of the listener. The listener's attention is solely focused on the 'soundscape', through which the language of the characters is necessarily foregrounded and where an otherworldly quality pervades. The radio medium, therefore, blurs the distinction between internal and external, between monologue and soliloquy. Remarking on the kinship between the radio medium and Beckett's literary interests at this stage of his career, Martin Esslin claims, 'It is precisely the nature of the radio medium which makes possible the fusion of an external dramatic action (as distinct from the wholly internalized monologues of the narrative trilogy which followed *Watt*) with its refraction and distortion in the mirror of a wholly subjective experience.'[14] In other words, Beckett's radio monologues can probe like his prose into the consciousness of the characters, while still maintaining the performative and dramatic quality of his plays. In all Beckett's plays, as we have seen, silence and pauses are a crucial part of the dramatic language. This is true of the stage but all the more so of the radio, where there are no visual stimuli to keep a listener involved. 'Silence is at the heart of the radio experience,'[15] stresses Donald McWhinnie, the producer of *All That Fall* and *Embers* on BBC radio.

All That Fall

Interestingly, the move to a new medium required a number of compensatory strategies to make up for the loss of the visual dimension. So *All That Fall* is Beckett's most realistic play, as if the grounding in a recognisable world makes up for the absence of a physical manifestation. Though it is far from straight naturalism, and while it is intensely aware of its own medium of transmission, the play has a level of plausibility in terms of plot, character-isation and language which most of Beckett's other plays lack. This is also reflected in a relatively high level of overt Irishness and autobiography in the play. Boghill is clearly based on Foxrock, the affluent commuter village outside Dublin where Beckett was brought up. There is still mystery and withheld information here. Whether Dan actually did push the child off the train at the end is not confirmed. The dialogue, for all its comically banal neighbourliness, is often strange and bleak and biblical. Idle chat about the races combines with Job-like curses of existence: Mr Tyler remarks to Mrs Rooney, 'I was merely cursing, under my breath, God and man, under my breath, and the wet Saturday afternoon of my conception' (15). But none-theless the characters here generally speak an everyday version of Irish-English, and their exchanges, though sometimes odd and discomfiting, place no great strain on credibility.

Despite the absence of visual imagery, this is Beckett's most teeming and lively play. There is far more to see and hear here than on the Beckett stage, though this plenitude is of course based on evocation not presentation. The auditory spectrum – cows, sheep, horses, trains and so on – evoke visual counterparts in the imagination of the listener. Often, and in line with that blurring in radio between the mind of a character and the outside world, our 'pictures' come from Maddy's own perspective. We imagine what she com-ments on and the sounds we hear are, generally, the sounds to which she attends, just as in *Embers* we only hear the sea when Henry cannot help himself from hearing it. This is one of the ways that these plays depart from objective naturalism and take on the perspective of the characters. 'Back-ground' sounds are never independent. A stage rendering of these plays would, obviously, destroy this perspective: we would see all the background ourselves and not be reliant on the thoughts of the character. Hence Beckett's persistent refusal to allow his radio plays to be performed on stage, including turning down a proposed staging of *All That Fall* with Laurence Olivier and Peggy Ashcroft. Insisting that the play not be performed on stage, he wrote to his American publisher Barney Rosset that whatever quality it has 'depends on the whole thing's coming out of the dark'.[16]

There is tension between the nature of the medium and the narrative it contains. The essence of radio is insubstantiality: the *air*waves are by defin-ition ephemeral. Yet, *All That Fall* gains its dramatic energy precisely by opposing this weightlessness with weight. The opening scene, with Maddy puffing and panting as she drags her heavy bulk towards the station, contrasts with the airiness of the radio medium: 'How can I go on, I cannot. Oh let me just flop down flat on the road like a big fat jelly out of a bowl and never move again! A great big slop thick with grit and dust and flies, they would have to scoop me up with a shovel' (14). Throughout her journey to the station Maddy's weightiness ('two hundred pounds of unhealthy fat,' remarks her husband later) is continually emphasised. The very title of *All That Fall* ties in with this theme of gravity and weight. We are given the biblical origin near the end by Dan: '"The Lord upholdeth all that fall and raiseth up all those that be bowed down"', a quotation that is greeted with 'wild laughter' from the old couple (38). Of course, a little later, when we learn of the child that has fallen (or been pushed) from the train, the titular quotation seems mordantly ironic: the Lord has not 'upheld' the child that fell from the train.

Along with the incorporation of weightiness, inertia and exertion – a stubborn and unmoving hinny, a deflated bicycle tyre, an unresponsive car engine, a late train – the play also deploys opposite notions of airiness and absence. On the radio, without a voice, a character's presence becomes far more uncertain than on stage. This is why Maddy feels so eager to assert her presence, when a conversation takes place without her: 'Do not imagine, because I am silent, that I am not present, and alive, to all that is going on' (25). A little earlier, she has snapped at the other characters, 'Don't mind me. Don't take any notice of me. I do not exist. The fact is well known' (19). The tetchiness of an aggrieved old woman is here refracted back as a comment on the radiogenic medium. At the same time it touches on the haziness of selfhood and identity that Beckett's work in prose and drama continually explores. This sense of not fully being there is not simply Maddy's problem. Miss Fitt, so alone with her 'Maker' in church, that she cannot see anyone or anything even after she leaves, confesses, 'I suppose the truth is I am not there, Mrs Rooney, just not really there at all' (22–3).

These allusions to a partial existence chime with the many references throughout the play to infertility, barrenness, early death and lost opportunities. 'Oh I am just a hysterical old hag I know, destroyed with sorrow and pining and gentility and churchgoing and fat and rheumatism and childlessness' (14). Maddy's sorrow and pining are focused on her thoughts of Minnie, her daughter, who died as a child: 'In her forties now she'd be, I don't know, fifty, girding up her lovely little loins, getting ready for the change' (16). Despite the farcical pastoralism of the setting and despite the comic depictions of Maddy's own sexual bawdiness with Slocum, we have a preoccupation with ill-health, arrested reproduction and childlessness. When Maddy inquires after Mr Tyler's daughter, he replies 'Fair, fair. They removed everything, you know, the whole . . . er . . . bag of tricks. Now I am grandchildless' (14). Has his daughter had a hysterectomy? Mr Tyler's hesitancy here, his search for a euphemism for his daughter's 'operation', gives a comically contrasting veneer of neighbourly respectability to the general obsession in the play with infertility, miscarriage and child death.

In the early 1960s, Beckett spoke to Lawrence Harvey about a general feeling of 'being absent' or 'existence by proxy'. Along with this sense of contingent or displaced experience goes the intuition of 'a presence, embryonic, undeveloped, of a self that might have been but never got born, an être manqué [an absent being].'[17] Given the preoccupation with absent presence in *All That Fall*, with characters who are not quite 'there', together with the associated theme of sterility and child death, these remarks are particularly illuminating. Harvey goes on to offer a reading of *All That Fall* in the light of his conversation with Beckett as 'a parable about this abortive being'.

> It is Minnie the little girl that Mrs Rooney lost. It is the dying child of whom the mind doctor says, 'The trouble with her was she had never really been born!' And finally, it is the little child that fell out of the train in which Mr Rooney was riding and disappeared under its wheels.[18]

These three dead children in the play, and the other references to infertility and miscarriage, reinforce a sense of ruptured possibility, of youth and promise pulled up short. In particular, Maddy's famous recollection of going to see one of those 'new mind doctors' (psychoanalysts) has sometimes been held up as a one of the most crucial lines in Beckett's work. The girl who has 'never really been born' incarnates very explicitly Beckett's sensation of existence by proxy, the feeling of a suspended or displaced being (36). There is an autobiographical correspondence for this incident in a lecture given by Carl Jung that Beckett attended in October 1935 in the company of his own analyst at the time, Dr W. R. Bion.[19] It seems to have struck Beckett forcefully as he also includes an allusion to it in the 'Addenda' to *Watt*, where the dislocated phrase 'never been properly born' sits in isolated significance (248). The description also haunts his 1976 play *Footfalls*. Beckett elaborated on the personal and intellectual resonance the Jung lecture had for him during a conversation with Charles Juliet in 1968:

> I have always sensed that there was within me an assassinated being. Assassinated before my birth. I needed to find this assassinated person again. And try to give him new life. I once attended a lecture by Jung in which he spoke about one of his patients, a very young girl. After the lecture, as everyone was leaving, Jung stood by silently. And then, as if speaking to himself, astonished by the discovery that he was making, he added: In the most fundamental way, she had never really been born. I too always had the sense of never having been born.[20]

At one level, the idea of never really being born has a relationship to 'original sin', a theological image that, as already seen, Beckett exploited in *Waiting for Godot* and elsewhere. There is an aboriginal 'flaw' in existence that comes along with birth itself. On the other hand, there is something in the concept of not being properly born, or of being assassinated before birth, which simultaneously brushes against this sort of fatalism, this idea of the irremediable. Whatever else the mysterious notion of not being properly born might mean it does highlight an absence, an imperfection in the self. And this immediately begs the question, what might a whole or an integrated self be like? We may not know the Godot who is missing in Beckett's world, no alternatives are offered to the curtailed existence depicted, but the shape left by his absence is hauntingly present. Similarly, the idea of being assassinated before birth, or of a murdered child, brings us toward a sense of loss and thwarted possibility that is the opposite of complacency or fatalism.

Embers

The feeling of being absent, of existence by proxy, about which Beckett spoke with Lawrence Harvey and which he deployed the radio medium to explore artistically, is elaborated in *Embers*, where the ghostliness and ephemerality of the characters is more emphasised. Henry may be a concrete figure, but Ada is tantalisingly ambiguous. An incorporeal, evanescent voice, she is caught somewhere between life and death. Beckett wanted to maintain the uncertainty. Billie Whitelaw reported that he had responded to the direct question 'Look, am I dead?' in reference to Ada and other characters with 'Let's just say you're not all there.'[21]

Henry orders the sounds we hear into existence. He works as a producer, getting sounds when he calls for them: horses' hooves, a drip, thuds. It is never easy. From the first he is forced to repeat his commands: 'Hooves! (*Pause. Louder.*) Hooves! (*Sound of hooves walking on hard road. They die rapidly away. Pause.*)'(93). It is uncertain here, even more than in *All That Fall*, whether the sounds are simply occurring in Henry's mind or whether they have some independent existence. Beckett said in an interview that '*Cendres* repose sur une ambiguité: le personage a-t-il une hallucination ou est-il en présence de la réalité? La réalisation scénique détruirait l'ambiguité.'[22] Henry's ability to produce sounds gets progressively worse until, towards the end of the play, he is no longer able to conjure up the hooves or have Ada speak to him. The relationship between his will, represented by language, and the ambiguous world surrounding him, represented by other sounds, has fissured. He is alone.

Corresponding to the spectrum between sound and silence, the characters often seem located somewhere between life and death, to a more intense degree than in *All That Fall*. Henry seems substantial and material. He makes sounds with his body when sitting down and standing up. Ada's voice, on the other hand, is 'low' and 'remote'; she makes no sound when sitting down on the shingle. Her auditory presence, therefore, has an eerie ghostlike quality. She seems suspended between life and death, reality and hallucination, between the outside world and Henry's feverish imaginings, between exteriority and interiority. Addie is even less present – we have her voice, evoked by Henry's memory – but she herself is suspiciously absent, revisiting the motif of the absent child deployed in *All That Fall*. The motif of infertility and unsatisfactory birth is here too, given how hard Addie was to conceive ('Years we kept hammering away at it' (101)) and how she was 'dragged' into this world. Like the earlier play, there is at least one allusion to miscarriage or, more accurately, abortion. Henry's robust father scorns his son as a 'washout' when he refuses to come for a 'dip' in the sea. 'Washout', ponders Henry, 'Wish to Christ she had', presumably wishing his mother had aborted him (96). Of course 'wash out' is exactly what happens to his father, who is lost at sea. This is not the only hint at suicide in the play: there is also the implication that in Henry's story what Bolton is pleading from the doctor, Holloway, is euthanasia of some sort.

That we do hear the voices of Ada and Addie makes the absence of Henry's father's voice all the more poignant. Henry is obsessed with his father. His father met his death on the sea, so for Henry it has become 'Some old grave I cannot tear myself away from' (98). At the beginning of the play Henry insists that his father is 'back from the dead' (93), but his non-presence haunts the rest of the performance, reinforcing the sense of loss and regret permeating Henry's reminiscences.

The story that Henry is endlessly telling about Bolton and Holloway is aimed to help him to escape the sound of the sea. Henry tells it in the present tense with continual improvisations, uttering a description, then changing it:

> There before the fire. (*Pause.*) Before the fire with all the shutters. . . no, hangings, hangings, all the hangings drawn and the light, no light, only the light of the fire, sitting there in the . . . no, standing, standing there on the hearthrug . . . (94)

This method is effective not only because it imparts the toil Henry has to invest to maintain the narrative but also because, like the radio medium itself, it is a process not a product. We tune into the story in the course of its transmission, which in Henry's case is equivalent to its creation. Crucially, unlike the scenes of Addie's distressful tutelage, the narrative is not evoked audibly. We rely entirely on Henry relating it to us. This reinforces the deathliness of the scene, particularly since the encounter between Bolton and Holloway is the most intensely visual in the play. 'Not a sound' is a constantly recurring phrase. There is one exception, a sound of dying embers, which he tries to make us hear but cannot project: 'not a sound, only the fire, no flames now, embers. (*Pause.*) Embers. (*Pause.*) Shifting, lapsing, furtive like, dreadful sound' (95). This sound – the title of the play – we are denied. To sound it would be to give it life, when it represents death and extinction. They may sound dreadful to Henry himself, but, as with the sound of the sea that he also reviles, the listener has a different impression. The encounter between Holloway and Bolton evokes a winter's night, with all outside cloaked in snow. Notwithstanding the desperation of Bolton's pleas, the scene is created through a beguilingly serene and rhythmic prose.

Embers differs from *All That Fall* in that behind the foreground sounds lies not silence but the ubiquitous sound of the sea. Henry yearns to escape from this desperate sound, which he describes as 'lips and claws' (98). The story of Bolton and Holloway, the various sounds he conjures, his attempt to talk to his dead father and his success in talking to his wife are a way of distracting himself from the sound of the sea, just as Vladimir and Estragon seek to avoid the dead voices. However, there is surely some ambivalence here. If Henry is only repelled by the sea, then why is he so physically drawn to it? Surely part of his fear of the sea comes from its powerful, siren-like attraction for him? Ada claims that 'it's a lovely peaceful gentle soothing sound' (100) and, crucially, it *is* perceived as such by the listener. The rhythmic, susurating whisper of breaking waves does not strike us as malevolent or threatening. It is a mesmerising sound for Henry too, despite his fear of it.

Krapp's Last Tape

Like most of the decrepit old creatures loitering on Beckett's stage, the eponymous hero of *Krapp's Last Tape* has only bemused contempt for abstract intellectual speculation or self-analysis. Alone in his den, fumbling through the tape made thirty years before on his thirty-ninth birthday, he thrice stumbles on the bombastic passage of his 'vision' at the end of the jetty, his revelation that 'the dark I have always struggled to keep under' would be the raw material of his art (60). This epiphany is greeted with curses and frustration by the elder Krapp, who has only a bitter laugh for the smug theorising of his younger self: 'Just been listening to that stupid bastard I took myself for thirty years ago, hard to believe I was ever as bad as that' (62). The passage he wants to hear is not the vision on the jetty, which gave him the literary vocation that he subsequently pursued, but the evocative, sensually depicted scene with the woman in the punt, the scene indexed in the ledger as 'Farewell to Love'. What interests him is not the road he followed in life, which has led him to his present moribund condition, but the road from which he turned. Clearly, like many of Beckett's plays, *Krapp's Last Tape* is concerned with the ravages of time. But, unlike many of the others this play deals not just with nostalgia and loss, but also with regret.

The rosy view many of Beckett's characters adopt towards the past often says more about the unreliability of voluntary memory, and the comparative dereliction of the present condition, than about what the past was actually like. 'Ah Yesterday!' Nell from *Endgame* repeatedly sighs in reflexive and uncritical nostalgia. The tapes in *Krapp's Last Tape* open a new dimension in the treatment of the past in Beckett's drama, for here we do not simply have the sepia-tinted past reconfigured to fit the needs of the present. Rather the voice is captured at the moment of recording, without all the distortions of retrospection. But the tape only preserves in the narrowest sense. It protects the memory of the years gone by, but in so doing it exacerbates the feeling of irreparable loss in the present. The preservation of time intensifies the consciousness of its passage.

It is not hard to see the influence of Beckett's forays into the radio medium in *Krapp's Last Tape*. He wanted to probe the dramatic impact of a disembodied voice on stage, having explored its possibilities over the airwaves in *All That Fall*. *Krapp's Last Tape* was originally called 'Magee Monologue', as it was written with the cracked voice of Patrick Magee, one of Beckett's favourite actors, in mind. Beckett had heard Magee read extracts from Beckett's *From an Abandoned Work* (written about 1954–5) on the BBC's Third Programme in December 1957. So from the beginning the play's inspiration was auditory, an influence that leaves its trace in the finished product. Using the tape recorder on stage brought the disembodied voice of the radio into the materiality of stage performance. But at the same time it solved the perennial problem of drama based on monologue: how can dramatic conflict be achieved? With the tape recorder, although only one person is on stage, the play manages in effect to have two psychologies. Beckett argued as long ago as *Proust* the radical effect that time has on the self. It is not just that *we* spend time; rather it spends *us*, rendering the individual fundamentally different to what it was: 'We are not merely more weary because of yesterday, we are other, no longer what we were before the calamity of yesterday' (P 13). Dramatic conflict is achieved by setting an individual against his past self, revealing in the process the distance and otherness that time and experience have generated.

The conflict, then, is between cynical and disillusioned older Krapp and the more hopeful man he was in early middle age. The difference is signalled not just by the older-sounding voice but also by the different languages used by the 'two' characters we hear, and the different psychologies these voices represent. Krapp the younger is more energetic and smugger: 'Thirty-nine today, sound as a bell, apart from my old weakness, and intellectually I have now every reason to suspect at the . . . (*hesitates*) . . . crest of a wave – or thereabouts' (57). Krapp the elder's language is starker and more fragmentary, reflecting his more derelict and enfeebled condition: 'What's a year now? The sour cud and the iron stool' (62). The younger man's vocabulary is more specialised and more arcane ('mother lay a-dying' (59)), too much sometimes for the older Krapp, who has to stop the tape to look up his dictionary when he hears the word 'viduity'. Yet at the same time as these differences in language and attitude create conflict, there are also repeated suggestions of continuity: the description of the den, the habit of eating bananas, drinking alcohol and so on. Krapp at sixty-nine can heartily join in with the recorded voice of Krapp at thirty-nine in laughing at the naivety and idealism of Krapp in his late twenties:

> Hard to believe I was ever that young whelp. The voice! Jesus! And the aspirations! (*Brief laugh in which* KRAPP *joins.*) And the resolutions! (*Brief laugh in which* KRAPP *joins.*) To drink less, in particular. (*Brief laugh of* KRAPP *alone.*)   (58)

Both Krapps can scorn the youthful aspirations and resolutions of their younger self, knowing just how futile they will prove to be. Only Krapp the elder laughs at the wish to drink less, presumably because middle-aged Krapp has not quite given up this resolution himself and is still trying to cut down on alcohol. As we can hear from Krapp the elder's cork-popping in the dark, he will not be successful. So, although the Krapps are different enough to create conflict, there are nonetheless deft and disconcerting continuities. Each likes to lambast the over-optimism and naivety of the younger self to whom he has just been listening. Even the young whelp in his late twenties, for all his optimism, 'Sneers at what he calls his youth and thanks to God that it's over' (58). It is a technique of rich and multiple irony, in which the middle-aged man derides his youthful ambitions and then, years later, derides the derider. The sheer disappointment of advancing age has rarely been dramatised with an economy that so satisfyingly combines poignancy and humour.

The *magnum opus* which Krapp finally got around to writing, perhaps making notes for it on his thirty-ninth birthday, turned out to be something of a failure in commercial terms: 'Seventeen copies sold, of which eleven at trade price to free circulating libraries beyond the seas' (62). The disappointing sales of Beckett's early publications, such as *Murphy*, spring to mind here. Krapp at thirty-nine regards the night of the 'Memorable Equinox', when he had his vision, as marking a creative epiphany. He must explore the darkness within him, rather than seek artistic material in the outside world. Perhaps his vision prompted him to turn his back on his romantic attachment, rejecting love and companionship to pursue the solitary life of the artist, a vocation which for him would require immersion in the self, in the dark he had strived to keep under. That 'Farewell to Love' comes just after 'Memorable Equinox' in the ledger would support this interpretation. The decision, retrospect reveals, brings him to an old age of obscurity, failure and loneliness.

But surely 'making the wrong decision' is far too worldly and avoidable to be the cause of unhappiness in Beckett's world? The misery that Hamm or the Unnamable suffers could hardly be explained in terms of some erroneous life choice. They would seem to be caught up in deterministic systems that squeeze out the possibility of human agency. Krapp's plight seems different. At least he had some control over his life. Yes, he turned down his chance of happiness, but at least he was given the choice. On the other hand, however, perhaps the burden of freedom makes things worse for Krapp. His torment made all the worse from knowing that it could have avoided, had he made a different decision. While the other characters have the solace of nostalgia, Krapp has the burden of regret.

Yet it would appear that regret is just as chimerical as nostalgia. In Beckett's world there is disappointment if one does not get what one wants, disillusionment if one does. Krapp may imagine a happy life in which he had not said farewell to love, but this is as delusory as the memories of an idyllic past with which some of Beckett's other characters console themselves. Beckett maintained that had Krapp taken the different route through life, chosen the girl and abandoned the *magnum opus*, his situation would be just as bad:

> I thought of writing a play on the opposite situation with Mrs Krapp, the girl in the punt, nagging away behind him in which case his failure and solitude would be exactly the same.[23]

Beckett seems determined not to allow a solution for the predicament of his characters. Their suffering, it seems, has no temporal or earthly way out, though some of them might delude themselves into thinking that if something were to happen in the future, if a Godot were to arrive or, in this case, if something different had happened in the past, that their plight would be relieved. The truth seems to be that, as Hamm declares, 'you're on earth, there's no cure for that' (37).

Many commentators have noted the importance of light and darkness, white and black, both as a structural device providing visual contrast, and as a metaphor for some of the play's central themes. Beckett pointed out to his American director that 'this simple antithesis' echoes 'throughout the text (black ball, white nurse, black pram, Bianca, Kedar – anagram of "dark" – Street, black storm, light of understanding etc. Black dictionary if you can and ledger. Similarly black and white set.'[24] The lighting of the play, with a strong white light on the table and the immediately adjacent area and the rest in darkness, contains and reinforces this motif. The thirty-nine-year-old Krapp says on the tape, 'The new light above my table is a great improvement. With all this darkness around me I feel less alone. (*Pause.*) In a way. (*Pause.*) I love to get up and move about in it, then back here to . . . (*hesitates*) . . . me. (*Pause.*) Krapp' (57). Coming back to the light indicates a return to self for Krapp, just as the playing of the old tapes is an attempt to recover the lost selves of previous years. They are, in a sense, a search for integrity, an attempt to heal the fissures in the self rendered by time.

So insistent is the light–dark opposition here that is has been regarded as emblematic of a fundamental dualism in the play.[25] Beckett's notes to the production of *Krapp's Last Tape* which he directed in the Schiller-Theater Werkstatt in Berlin in 1969 are unusually explicit about the matter, elaborating a Manichaean series of oppositions around light and dark. Beckett is clearly well versed in Manichaean theology and identifies light/white in the play as 'spiritual' and black/darkness as 'sensual'. Manichaean belief (deriving from the teachings of Mani, a third-century Iranian theologian) holds that the world is caught in an unholy blending of good and evil, and the duty of the faithful is, through a renunciation of the ways of the flesh, to liberate the imprisoned light or goodness from its debased entrapment in the evil world of matter. There are three or four pages of elaboration on this Manichaean dimension to the play in Beckett's production notebook. It is rare for him to provide so full an intellectual frame for reading a play, but James Knowlson is surely right to advise caution. Beckett intimated that he himself only discovered the Manichaean dimension to the play when he came to direct it – some eleven years after he wrote it. If this is so, then the variations of black and white were presumably first used, at least on the conscious level, for dramatic contrast and shape, rather than as an intellectual or theological allegory.

Nonetheless, the Manichaean production notes are tantalising. They suggest that the 'sin' for which Krapp is punished is the 'reconciliation' of light and dark 'intellectually as rational-irrational'. Krapp turns from 'fact of anti-mind alien to mind' to the 'thought of anti-mind constituent of mind'. The images of merging of light and dark, white and black that occur throughout the play represent this transgressive integration. Remembering the events surrounding the death of his mother, Krapp on the tape recollects a nurse in white starched clothes with a black perambulator ('most funereal thing') and a white dog to whom he gives a 'small, old, black, hard, solid rubber ball. (*Pause.*) I shall feel it, in my hand, until my dying day. (*Pause.*) I might have kept it. (*Pause.*) But I gave it to the dog' (60). The incident, particularly the significance with which it is imbued here, has been much considered by critics. Beckett, in his production notebook, ties it to the Manichaean schema: 'Note that if the giving of the black ball to the white dog represents the sacrifice of sense to spirit the form here too is that of a mingling.'[26]

This mingling of white and black, light and dark, spirit and sensuality is Krapp's offence in a Manichaean world with an ethic of ascetic separation of spirit from sensuality, mind from non-mind. Perhaps the central instance of this 'offence' takes place during his 'vision' on the jetty. This moment is explicitly about the merging of light and dark, the rational and the irrational:

> Spiritually a year of profound gloom and indigence until that memorable night in March, at the end of the jetty, in the howling wind, never to be forgotten, when suddenly I saw the whole thing. The vision at last. This I fancy is what I have chiefly to record this evening, against the day when my work will be done and perhaps no place left in my memory, warm or cold, for the miracle that . . . (*hesitates*) . . . for the fire that set it alight. What I suddenly saw then was this, that the belief I had been going on all my life, namely – (KRAPP *switches off impatiently, winds tape forward, switches on again*) – great granite rocks the foam flying up in the light of the lighthouse and the wind-gauge spinning like a propeller, clear to me at last that the dark I have always struggled to keep under is in reality my most – (60)

Clarity here merges with impenetrability, the light from the lighthouse beams into the darkness of the night, the 'fire' that set his vision 'alight' mingles with darkness he has 'kept under'. All these metaphors betoken his decision to incorporate the non-rational, non-enlightened, non-verbal aspects of his psyche – the dark he struggled to keep under – into his art. Presumably the *magnum opus* that springs from this vision, like Beckett's post-war prose, turns away from erudition and omnipotence towards an art of ignorance and impotence. For the purposes of *Krapp's Last Tape*, however, the choice is an ethical abnegation, a sin for which, according to Beckett's Manichaean production notebook, 'he is punished as shown by the aeons'.[27]

Unlike in later plays like *Happy Days* or *Play*, where the light overhead is explicitly part of the torment, light is a comparatively benign presence in *Krapp's Last Tape*. As already seen, Krapp at thirty-nine likes to leave the light and venture into the dark, so he can have the satisfaction of returning to the protective light. Though Krapp's situation is desolate and without promise for the future, one could make a case that this is Beckett's most tender, humane and poignant play. Whereas in *Endgame* the very values which might make loss tragic have themselves been lost, here there is a real sense that the missed opportunities of a wasted life are worth mourning. There is a certain wintry consolation in the recognition that the devastation visited on Krapp actually means something. This is reflected in the language, particularly the scene with the girl in the punt, which Krapp deems worth listening to twice:

> I said again I thought it was hopeless and no good going on and she agreed, without opening her eyes. (*Pause.*) I asked her to look at me after a few moments – (*Pause.*) – after a few moments she did, but the eyes just slits because of the glare. I bent over to get them in the shadow and they opened. (*Pause. Low.*) Let me in. (*Pause.*) We drifted in among the flags and stuck. The way they went down, sighing, before the stem! (*Pause.*) I lay down across her with my face in her breasts and my hand on her. We lay there without moving. But under us all moved, and moved us, gently, up and down, and from side to side.   (63)

Even though this scene describes the moment, thirty years before, when the listener set himself on course for his present wretchedness, the economy and delicacy of the description here produces a rare and moving beauty. So many moods commingle: the abjectness of Krapp's current condition, the confident tone of his younger self, the sadness of the two departing lovers. But all are suffused with the gentleness of the floating barge, the intimacy of the lovers within. Beckett commented to James Knowlson, 'if you take a single syllable out of those lines, you destroy the sound of the lapping water on the side of the boat'.[28] Beckett's mature writing is never indulgent, it never gluts on description or verbosity. The pleasure it produces comes from its utter precision and economy, using the minimum of words to maximum effect. It thrives on an aesthetic of depletion and frugality, which is why his works tend to get ever shorter as his career advances. Therefore, a lyrical passage such as Krapp on the barge strikes us with special power. Despite Krapp's pitiful condition now, with only death to await him, the beauty of the language and the authenticity of the feeling here give this play, unlike many of the others, a certain fragile affirmation.

Happy Days

The settings of *Krapp's Last Tape* or *Waiting for Godot* or even that of *Endgame* may be strange, unlikely and alienating. But they are not entirely implausible. There are still a few frayed threads connecting these scenarios to a believable world, albeit one that is depleted, atrophied and shot through with negation. *Happy Days* marks a radical severance with even the residual feasibility that existed in Beckett's early drama. This is not to say that there are not many elements of the play that connect to a realistic context – the play has an unusually large investment in the detritus of everyday life. But the central theatrical image on which the play is based, in which a seemingly cheerful woman is progressively and helplessly absorbed into a mound of earth while her husband reads the newspaper beside her, is not one which we are likely to see too often in actual experience. It is, nonetheless, an intense theatrical metaphor, wonderfully providing a scenic counterpoint to the optimistic prattle of Winnie's garrulous speeches.

Her story of the man and the woman (Shower or Cooker) who, passing by, speculate as to why she is there and why Willie does not dig her out, is a knowing nod at the oddness of her situation. The passing couple adopt the same perplexity in the face of this bizarre situation as an anticipated audience might. Beckett leaves the cause of Winnie's confinement as indeterminate as that of the devastation that precedes *Endgame* or the motive that brings Vladimir and Estragon to their appointment with Godot. Her memories suggest that she has not always been confined to this mound of earth, that she used to have the use of her legs, so when in the second act she is buried still deeper in the mound, now up to her neck, it becomes apparent that her immersion in the earth, like the degenerative aspect of life itself, is inevitable and progressive. But, as ever in Beckett, though the metaphor gestures towards the destructiveness of time, it cannot simply be hammered into an unbending allegory.

Her immersion in the earth is not the end of Winnie's troubles. She is also exposed to a 'hellish light' that pins her from above just as the ground grasps her from below. In *Endgame* light was life-giving (Mother Pegg died of darkness), though this was no unqualified blessing. Now it is a torment. There is no escape from the glare, no dimness in which she can gain relief.

Even the parasol she strives to use for this purpose catches fire, presumably as a result of the heat. Winnie is roused from the solace of sleep by a loud and protracted bell ring. Ironically the bright and sunny setting, together with the parasol, the newspaper and Willie's handkerchief, can momentarily come to resemble a day at the seaside, though of course the sea seems far from this desolate desert. Seaside resorts were once notorious for saucy pictures, in Britain at least. When Willie allows her to examine his postcard, she exclaims: 'Heavens what are they up to! (*She looks for spectacles, puts them on and examines card.*) No but this is just genuine pure filth! (*Examines card.*) Make any nice-minded person want to vomit!' (16). Her desperate need to keep up a veneer of normality, even propriety, is one of the darkly comic contrasts around which the play hinges.

The chief such is, of course, the disjunction between Winnie's optimistic tone and the (literal) gravity of her situation. It is not unusual for Beckett's stage characters to distract themselves with stories or recounted memories, but hitherto most of them have taken a pretty desolate view of life. Even the anti-intellectual Estragon's outbursts recognise the bleakness of his condition: 'Recognize! What is there to recognize? All my lousy life I've crawled about in the mud! And you talk to me about scenery! (*Looking wildly about him.*) Look at this muckheap! I've never stirred from it!' (61). They sometimes strive not to face up to their existence but they do not deny its awfulness. Winnie, on the other hand, needs to maintain a desperate cheeriness: 'Another heavenly day' are her first words, having been roused from her sleep by the piercing bell (9). Her speeches are peppered with optimistic little banalities: 'That is what I find so wonderful', 'great mercies', 'so much to be thankful for', 'this will have been another happy day' and so forth. It is a heavenly day despite the 'blaze of hellish light' that she inadvertently mentions a little later (11). Winnie lives in her mound as if she were domiciled in suburbia and her rituals of washing her teeth, cleaning her glasses, brushing her hair and so on seem on one level a normal morning routine, fairly at odds with the abnormality of the rest of her situation. Her morning grooming at the start of the play operates in comic contrast to her dire situation, but we might also be tempted to see extra significance here. Half buried in sand, Winnie looks herself like a tooth, a hair, a nail, or indeed one of the 'hog's setae' that make up the bristles on her toothbrush. Therefore banal activity like brushing teeth or hair operates simultaneously as an act of, and a metaphor for, self-grooming. Like the obsessive neurotic who continually scrubs and cleans as a displacement activity for a deeper disturbance, her self-grooming is a very vivid example of her need to distract herself from her terminal helplessness.

Like Estragon and Vladimir, like Hamm and Clov, she too must pass the time, fill in the day from morning to night. Winnie has two means of keeping going, the same two as Vladimir and Estragon: talking and doing. When talking breaks down, she reaches for her handbag, which in turn gives her a pretext for more talk:

> What now? (*Pause.*) Words fail, there are times when even they fail.
> (*Turning a little towards* WILLIE.) Is that not so, Willie? (*Pause. Turning a little further.*) Is that not so, Willie, that even words fail, at times? (*Pause. Back front.*) What is one to do then, until they come again? Brush and comb the hair, if it has not been done, or if there is some doubt, trim the nails if they are in need of trimming, these things tide one over.   (20)

Here is a distilled articulation of some of the play's major themes: Winnie's loneliness, her optimism, her clichéd tone, her need for connection. When words fail her, actions and routines can block out reality until she is allowed to sleep again. The focus on her moving arms and hands in the first act turns to her darting eyes in the second, a vivid theatrical image for her impairment. It is a serious challenge for any actress to keep the dramatic focus by the use only of her words and her eyes.

In many respects, however, and against those commentators who regard this as Beckett's most 'cheerful' play, she faces even more difficulties. Most obviously, her physical debilitation and immobility is more extensive than any of the others – at least Hamm has his gaff. In the second act she is almost totally immobilised, anticipating later Beckett plays like *Play* or *Not I*. Second, her need to be cheerful does not make her plight easier or more uplifting, it actually makes it worse. Hamm can at least rail against his father or his God; Krapp can scornfully cackle at his younger self, but poor Winnie does not have the inverted consolations that disillusionment or cynicism can offer. She has to maintain her ever-more fragile cheeriness no matter how awful the circumstances. 'Can't complain', she chirpily gasps, as the very earth around her sucks her in. Unlike, say, *Waiting for Godot*, the day here does not end. There are no stage directions to dim the 'hellish' light and the noonday sun, glaring and intrusive, will not pale. Whenever Winnie uses the word 'day', she adds the phrase 'to speak in the old style'. The concept of day and night has left this world of endless glare. We see Winnie waking up at the start of both acts but, significantly, we never see her going to sleep. She sees Willie do so, seemingly at will, which she regards as 'a marvellous gift' (11). If she tries too hard to avoid the light, the bell comes to upbraid her. It rouses her when she threatens to drift into sleep in the first act, but it stops her from even closing her eyes in the second. 'It hurts like a knife. (*Pause.*) A gouge.

(*Pause.*) One cannot ignore it' (40). The light here enforces one of the key motifs of the play, that of violation and intrusion.

Finally, and importantly, what makes life worse for Winnie, unlike the comic pairings of Beckett's fifties' drama, is the frailty of her companionship. Sadly for her, she has a much less cooperative partner with whom to play verbal and physical games. He answers her only sporadically and typically in monosyllables. Until he crawls round to the front of the mound near the end of the play, we do not see his face. Yet, despite his inadequacies, her need for him is desperate, though she wishes she did not need a listener for her chatter: 'Ah yes, if only I could bear to be alone, I mean prattle away with not a soul to hear. (*Pause.*) Not that I flatter myself you hear much, no Willie, God forbid' (18). She cannot bear to be alone, to be without a listener, but poignantly enough she knows that her husband hardly listens to her inane chatter. It is an unexpected and delightful boon if he chooses to actually respond to her.

All dramatic performance must at some level draw from cultural codes, prejudices, ideologies, whether it deploys, subverts or reinforces them. Part of the experience of watching a play is the experience of recognition – this often comes from there being a recognisable 'type' on stage. Beckett's fame is typically that of an innovator who tends to thwart the urge for comfortable recognition in his audiences. However, for the estranging experience of a Beckett play to effectively claw, it has to be juxtaposed with shards of familiarity. So, for instance, for all the oddness of Winnie's predicament, there is an ordinariness to her routine. To the extent that *Happy Days* has to do with marriage, it exploits and indeed parodies a stereotype in which a woman talks incessantly while a husband sits apart reading the newspaper, emitting the odd grunt or, very occasionally, offering one-syllable answers. One could accuse the play of a sexist depiction of a gabbling, middle-aged wife, full of neurotically fragile optimism, if the stereotype was not so remorselessly exaggerated and sent up. Nonetheless, it is worth bearing in mind that the play keys into a recognisable discourse of gender that would be lost if, say, Willie was chattering in the mound and Winnie reading the paper. It also, one could argue, plays off recognisable discourses of class and nationality. The pair – and their costumes alone signal this – are clearly middle-class, faintly outdated party-goers. Winnie's optimism also exploits a certain discourse of resilient Englishness, cheery and good-humoured regardless of the tribulations. 'It is a curiously *English* play', according to Hugh Kenner: 'the unquestioning assumption that the warp and woof of an unfulfilling day consist in maintaining one's cheer is a premise of English gentility as perhaps no other.'[29]

Prose works

More Pricks than Kicks

More Pricks than Kicks, a collection of ten short stories, was Beckett's first book-length publication of fiction. The title combines a biblical allusion ('It is hard for thee to kick against the pricks', Acts 26: 14) with an obscene pun. Like so much of Beckett's work, the collection is rich in biblical and religious allusion. Since much of the collection is given over to its hero's encounters with women, the sexual overture is appropriate. This mixture of the sacred and the profane, the spiritual and the bodily, is a common motif throughout the collection. These ten short stories feature Belacqua Shuah, a down-at-heel Trinity College student in his various misadventures around Dublin. Belacqua is named after a character in Dante's *Purgatorio* IV, who is detained in ante-purgatory for the sins of indolence and sloth, characteristics not entirely alien to the late-rising young Beckett. 'Shuah' is the mother of Onan (Genesis 38: 7–9) whose name gives us 'Onanism' or masturbation. The collection opens with the hero musing over a passage from *The Divine Comedy*. Throughout the stories there is a strong concentration on the topographical details of Dublin city and its environs.

Much of the material, such as the stories 'A Wet Night' and 'The Smer-aldina's Billet-Doux', was salvaged from his first novel, *Dream of Fair to Middling Women*, unpublished during Beckett's own lifetime. For all the heavy formal experimentalism, arcane allusion and fluidity of narrative perspective of the original novel, these stories tend to adopt a more conventional third-person distance between the narrator and the characters, though the narrative voice maintains some of the original pedantry. They rely on a recognisable plot, character interaction is coherent, and the relationship between cause and effect is generally clear. The motivations of Belacqua (the only character who is developed) are unmasked, even if they often appear eccentric or odd. Despite the relative conventionality of narrative perspective, the stories are written in a highly erudite prose and rely for their effect on comically grotesque situations and darkly bizarre characterisation. The tone of the narrator is supercilious and often sardonic and overly mannered. The stories follow Belacqua through his daily life, his many diversions into the pub, his romantic encounters, his marriage, and his death on the operating table in the story 'Yellow'. They are thus linked together, not least by the character Belacqua, as their origin in the novel form would suggest, but each also has its own rationale and integrity. Comparisons with James Joyce's *Dubliners*, which also treats religion, drink and the search for independence, might seem tempting. But Beckett's baroque, allusive, intertextual style owes more to the later Joyce than to the 'scrupulous meanness' with which Joyce mastered the short story form. The tone and style of *More Pricks than Kicks* are a long way from the absolute economy and minimalism of Beckett's later prose works. To be sure, the collection often uses the understatement of the short story form when it comes to events of great significance – the death of Belacqua is told with notable nonchalance, for instance. However, in Beckett's case the casual rendering of crucial detail is accompanied by a heavily encrusted, epigrammatic cleverness on the part of the narrative voice. In the Joycean short story economy of detail cracks open a shaft of illumination, an 'epiphany' that operates as a sort of climax to each of the stories. Beckett deploys parody and a heavily exhausted syntax to weigh down any such revelatory peak. Near the end of 'A Wet Night', there is a passage that unmistakably deflates the famous ending of Joyce's 'The Dead':

> But the wind had dropped, as it so often does in Dublin when all the respectable men and women whom it delights to annoy have gone to bed, and the rain fell in a uniform, untroubled manner. It fell upon the bay, the littoral, the mountains and the plains, and notably upon the Central Bog it fell with rather desolate uniformity.   (87)

The climax of 'The Dead', with the prose as delicate as the snowfall it describes, is here replaced with the cynical, lacklustre picture of rainfall, flatly described without significance or symbolism. It is a long way from Joyce's attempt to write a chapter in the moral history of his native city.

The first and most well-known story from the collection, 'Dante and the Lobster', begins with its hero deep in study. The concern switches quickly from the mind to the body, from the profound to the mundane, as he sets about organising his day. He has three tasks: organising his lunch, obtaining lobster for his evening meal with his aunt and attending his piano lesson. In his prize-winning poem 'Whoroscope' Beckett recalls Descartes's reputation for eating rotten eggs. Belacqua has a comparable dietary foible in the preparation of his lunch – blackened toast burned through at a low heat, smeared with mustard and topped off with carefully rotten Gorgonzola:

> He rubbed it. It was sweating. That was something. He stopped and smelt it. A faint fragrance of corruption. What good was that? He didn't want fragrance, he wasn't a bloody gourmet, he wanted a good stench. What he wanted was a good green stenching rotten lump of Gorgonzola cheese, alive, and by God he would have it. (13–14)

The narrative voice here is omniscient and ironic. Yet it is also faintly exhausted and impatient with the trivia it explores. The comic effect of the story stems from the mixture of the derelict and the punctilious, the squalid and the profound. This will be a common juxtaposition in Beckett's writings, which will later blur the distinction between the tramp and the seer, and it is often deployed, as here, for comic effect. Belacqua enters the shop looking like a vagabond, but views the grocer with the haughtiness of the most sneering toff. 'God damn these tradesmen, he thought, you can never rely on them' (16).

For all his indolence, Belacqua shares with many of Beckett's later characters a love of system and sequence. He wants to organise his day – lunch, lobster, piano lesson – in an ordered and regimented manner and is impatient of interruptions. Though he embraces his solitude and isolation, much of the collection is given over to sexual advances on him by various women. But Belacqua is an obersver, an outsider, and his preferred sexual activity is voyeurism, as we discover in the sixth story in the collection, 'Walking Out'. He dreams also in this story of being cuckolded by his betrothed, Lucy, so that he can be relieved of his conjugal duties. But shortly after discovering her husband's 'creepy-crawly' tendencies, Lucy is hit by a limousine, crippled for life and later dies.

Belacqua scampers for privacy and autonomy, yet is beset by physical, sexualised women. He escapes from one woman in 'Fingal' by pedalling away on a stolen bicycle when her attentions are elsewhere. Even in 'Yellow' the nurses attending him prevail upon him. Intellectual man beset by physical woman is a recurring model in Beckett's prose from *Murphy* to *Molloy* and beyond.

Murphy

Murphy is often the first encounter readers have with Beckett's fiction. The oddness of its characterisation and the dense eccentricity of style do not prevent it from having a relatively conventional plot and structure. Conventional, that is, insofar as its structure relies on exposition, complication and dénouement, in that it belongs to a recognisable tradition of the 'novel-of-ideas', in that there are recognisable characters performing determinate actions towards recognisable – if perplexing – ends. That which is conventional in the novel is, however, tremendously tied up in parody. There are disruptions to its narrative expectation, such as the notorious Chapter 6, outlining the contents of Murphy's 'mind'. And the novel is dense in philosophical and theological allusion. Occasionally the narrative comments on itself, in typical modernist self-reflexivity, apologising for its digressions and highlighting its own methods. Elsewhere, it is a pausing, self-conscious, mannered style, typical of the decadent modernism of the 1930s:

> Miss Counihan sat on Wylie's knees, *not* in Wynn's Hotel lest an action for libel should lie, and oyster kisses passed between them. Wylie did not often kiss, but when he did it was a serious matter. He was not one of those lugubrious persons who insist on removing the clapper from the bell of passion. A kiss from Wylie was like a breve tied, in a long slow amorous phrase, over bars' times its equivalent in demi-semiquavers. Miss Counihan had never enjoyed anything quite so much as this slow-motion osmosis of love's spittle.   (83)

At least three metaphors and one extravagant musical simile are used here to indicate Wylie and Miss Counihan's slow and wet kissing. The comic effect comes from the anomaly between the excessively scholastic and figuratively indulgent language and the rather squalid, tawdry subject matter. It is a common enough technique in this phase of Beckett's career. *Murphy* has a similarly recondite and sardonic, but much less mannered, tone to *Dream of Fair to Middling Women*. The learning and erudition here are more ironically deployed than in the earlier work. The jokes here are less encrusted with self-conscious display, though not yet entirely free from it, and there is far more intimation of Beckett's mature style. Later, Beckett will reject the language of philosophy and ratiocination altogether for a first-person prose of impotence and ignorance. At this stage, he parodies and mocks them in a burlesque, grotesque and comic novel, which (if it seems amongst the more accessible of Beckett's prose works in retrospect) was regarded as so obscure that it went through forty-two publishers' rejections before finally being accepted by

Routledge. The novel sold poorly initially, but benefited from a wave of retrospective interest following the success of *Waiting for Godot* some fifteen years later. In one sense it is easier than the bewildered musings of Beckett's post-war first-person narrators. However, for all its parody, it is a novel which often wears its learning prominently on its sleeve.

Murphy's route to mental peace is described early in the novel. He ties himself naked into his rocking chair and rocks until his body is 'appeased', after which, we are told, it will be possible for him to come alive in his mind 'as described in section six'. How he can bind himself so securely without the aid of another is not explained. He is only able to answer the telephone with great difficulty when it rings, so one might wonder how he went about tying his hands to the back of the chair without having someone else there to help him. This is one of the small departures from realism, or the plausible, in a novel which, though broadly realist, is full of the grotesque, the heavily farcical and the seriously trivial. In this first episode we also learn in flashback something about Murphy's background, specifically his erstwhile interest in Miss Counihan. We learn about Neary, another overly erudite oddball, to whom Murphy seems to have been apprenticed at one stage. Neary is capable of stopping his heart at will and, it seems, is more attached to the idea of love than Murphy. He represents a move towards the body, while Murphy seeks to move away from it – a key opposition in the novel.

Celia, the person at the other end of the phone when it disturbs Murphy's trance, is described minutely in Chapter 2 – Celia (*s'il y a* – 'if there is') represents that bodily actuality that counters Murphy's desire to escape the physical. It is significant, therefore, that our initial introduction to her is as a table of physical qualities, as a body broken down into its constituent parts duly measured. This reification of Celia, this transformation of her into quantifiable parts, is appropriate because of the actuality she represents but also points at her profession as a prostitute. She quite reasonably wants Murphy to get a job, not least because a return to her own profession will, she thinks, spell the end of her relationship with him. Murphy, however, in an inversion of the Protestant work ethic, has a horror of work bordering on the religious. This would involve a participative role in the world of paid labour that is degrading, an abnegation of his duty to self-realisation and mental escape. He lives on 'small charitable sums' derived, it turns out, from an uncle to whom, by arrangement with Murphy, the landlady submits fraudulent accounts. Murphy's ethics are the existentialist ones of authenticity and truth to himself, not the bourgeois ones of duty, thrift and self-reliance.

Murphy's lack of interest in the external, peopled world becomes more appropriate in the context of the novel, in which the peripheral characters are comically conniving, self-pitying, sexually appetitive, yet at the same time incongruously formal and formulaic. As the narrator notes, 'All the puppets in this book whinge sooner or later, except Murphy, who is not a puppet' (86).

Neary loves Miss Counihan, whose heart is on the absent Murphy. Neary reckons that, if he can prove that Murphy is not the success abroad that she supposes, but is rather a layabout, he will be able to free up her affections for him. So he sends his lackey, Cooper (the least socially exalted of the characters), to London to track down the luckless Murphy. Cooper fails, but the aptly named Wylie (another admirer of Miss Counihan) proposes that Neary himself goes to London in pursuit of Murphy, hence leaving the way free for Wylie himself to make his own advances on her.

In the second half of the novel, Murphy finds a different route to insight. Browbeaten by Celia into getting a job, he becomes a male nurse in the Magdalen Mental Mercyseat Hospital. His ethic of withdrawal and self-containment, the spurning of the world, is wonderfully embodied in the patients:

> They caused Murphy no horror. The most easily identifiable of his immediate feelings were respect and unworthiness [. . .] the impression he received was of the self-immersed indifference to the contingencies of the contingent world which he had chosen for himself as the only felicity and achieved so seldom.   (117)

Murphy's most persistent ambition has been to cut himself adrift from his unsatisfactory body and float off into the silent inner world of the mind. His admiration turns to awe in the face of one patient in particular, Mr Endon, with whom he develops a 'relationship', if a one-way fascination without any communication can be so described. They play day-long, silent, unfinished games of chess, but, to Murphy's satisfaction and envy, there is no interaction in these games, despite Murphy's attempts to draw his opponent out. The chess game they play, reproduced in Chapter 11, is one in which Mr Endon elaborately develops his pieces and then elaborately brings them back to a starting point, seemingly indifferent to the fact that he is playing a game with another person. It is a level of autonomy and disconnection with the world that Murphy admires and envies.

Murphy's interest in Mr Endon, though comic in parts, is entirely consistent with a crucial facet of his disposition and of the novel generally: his infatuation with closed systems. On the one hand Murphy is looking for 'freedom'; on the other, however, he is obsessed by deterministic patterns of one sort of another. Astronomy and astrology, so crucial to Murphy's sense of the world and sense of his own future, are part of this interest. Freedom and confinement are mutually linked in Murphy's worldview. He wants freedom for the mind, and as a counterpoint to this seeks restriction for the body by binding himself in ropes and moving backward and forward in his chair. Less obviously, but just as important as this physical restriction, is his eschewal of choice. He is continually looking to the zodiac to explain and to choose. It is his horoscope that decides whether he will accept Ticklepenny's offer of a job in the asylum, for instance.

The narrator also makes repeated reference to the cosmos, reinforcing the impression that the characters are caught up in some larger system of celestial control. The deterministic note is signalled in the famous first line: 'The sun shone, having no alternative, on the nothing new' (5). The novel is replete with repetitive devices: repeated passages, recurring episodes, characters with similar traits, various symmetries and patterns.[1] Of course, since they are already written, all novels are in one sense pre-determined narratives or closed systems. The pages which have yet to be turned also contain 'nothing new'. 'Something is taking its course,' as Clov will later say in *Endgame*. But this novel has a deliberately diagrammatic quality which intensifies this sense of predestination. It is as if it is working on mechanical or clockwork principles, a motif picked up in a number of exchanges. 'Somewhere a cuckoo-clock, having struck between twenty and thirty, became the echo of a street-cry, which now entering the mew gave *Quid pro quo! Quid pro quo!* directly!' (5). 'Quid pro quo', one thing standing in for another, a system of exchange, is pervasive both as a metaphor and a technique in the novel. So, for instance, we have the comic parody of romantic love, deeply unrequited but wrought into a symmetrical and ultimately circular system:

> Of such was Neary's love for Miss Dwyer, who loved a Flight-Lieutenant Elliman, who loved a Miss Farren of Ringsakiddy, who loved a Father Fitt of Ballinclashet, who in all sincerity was bound to acknowledge a certain vocation for a Mrs West of Passage, who loved Neary.   (7)

This parody of Romantic courtship, with all its fastidious delicacy of phrasing ('bound to acknowledge a certain vocation'), is only one example of closed systems. From Murphy's rocking chair to the game of chess he plays with Mr Endon, the narrative is fascinated with cycles and circularity of various sorts. And, as already argued, this picks up on the preset, repetitive nature of day-to-day life ('The sun having no alternative . . .') and the pre-determined quality of the novel form. A comparable interest in repetition, entrapment and determinism will haunt Beckett's post-war drama.

The concern with determinism also leads to an interest in the automated and scientific, both literally and metaphorically. The languages of physics, chemistry, medicine and mathematics are brought to bear on human experience. They are all evident in Wylie's fatalistic pronouncement:

> 'I greatly fear', said Wylie, 'that the syndrome known as life is too diffuse to admit of palliation. For every symptom that is eased, another is made worse. The horse leech's daughter is a closed system. Her quantum of wantum cannot vary.' (43)

'Life' is the 'syndrome' of a disease that cannot be cured. The level of human yearning ('the quantum of wantum') is irreducible because, as Beckett has argued in philosophical terms in his *Proust*, the root of desire, generated by a fissure in the self, is ultimately insatiable. In *Waiting for Godot*, Pozzo expresses a similar idea of human suffering caught up in a system of endless exchange: 'The tears of the world are a constant quantity. For each one who begins to weep, somewhere else another stops. The same is true of the laugh' (33). It is a curiously pessimistic and avowedly anti-political position. If life cannot be palliated then there is little point in trying to improve it by social or political means. But if it is ostensibly anti-political in its fatalistic attitude to suffering, it cannot be described as apolitical in its phrasing. The passage deploys an explicitly economic (and hence political) idiom of exchange, continuity and substitution.

Many commentators have pointed out that Murphy's view of the world is fundamentally dualistic, divided according to the mind and the body, spirit and matter, self and non-self. It is to the former that Murphy is drawn, away from the base, corporeal material world. The thinker most associated with dualism is seventeenth-century French philosopher René Descartes (1596–1650), and critics of *Murphy* have long pointed out this influence on the novel.[2] Descartes theorised that the mind and body are distinct, but not wholly separate. He posited that the pineal gland or the 'conarium' was the point in the physical brain which mediated between body and mind. But Neary tells Murphy early in the novel that his 'conarium has shrunk to nothing' (8), while in *More Pricks than Kicks*, Belacqua 'scoffed at the idea of a sequitur from his body to his mind' (31). It seems as if Murphy's dualism is more radical than Descartes's, allowing no physical connection between the two realms of mind and body. He appears to be a disciple of the post-Cartesian philosopher Arnold Geulincx (1624–69), whose works Beckett read avidly. Geulincx argued that mind and body are wholly separate, and that they only cooperate as a result of God's intervention. The mind does not instruct the foot to walk. Rather, the idea of walking enters the mind, which is the *occasion* for God to cause the motion of walking. There is no inherent connection in human terms between both events. Murphy is thus what philosophers call an *Occasionalist*, who considers his mind to be 'bodytight':

> Murphy felt himself split in two, a body and a mind. They had
> intercourse apparently, otherwise he could not have known they had
> anything in common. But he felt his mind to be bodytight and did not
> understand through what channel the intercourse was effected nor how
> the two experiences came to overlap. He was satisfied that neither
> followed from the other. He neither thought a kick because he felt one
> nor felt a kick because he thought one.   (77)

In other words the kick happens in two realms: the body and the mind. The two
are separate. How, then, are they related, if at all? Is there a third kick, which
connects the two, doing the work ascribed to God by Geulincx? 'Perhaps the
knowledge was related to the fact of the kick as two magnitudes to a third.
Perhaps there was, outside space and time, a non-mental, non-physical Kick
from all eternity' (77). But whereas the Occasionalists assigned to God the role of
the pineal gland, Murphy's dualism is shorn of divine intention. In God's place
Murphy puts in the astrological systems of Pandit Suk, the only system outside
his own in which he felt the least confidence, that of the 'heavenly bodies'. But the
difference between Geulincx's God and Murphy's planets is that the latter are
without any providential control. They operate according to a pattern, certainly,
but it is a pattern without a goal, determinism without *telos*. The sun has no
alternative but to shine on the nothing new, though it is to no greater good that
it does so. This is a clockwork universe, cold, mechanical, Godless.

   Again there is an intimation here of Beckett's later work, in which things
take their course in a world shaped around an absence where, in Western
civilisation, God used to be. Murphy still maintains the tenets of the Occasionalist doctrine, without the role of God. He also maintains the quietist
ethical system of this philosophy, based on renunciation of worldly pleasures.
Where one can do nothing (our will is simply the occasion for God's will, the
Occasionalists would maintain), one should renounce the worldly motives of
action, to retire within the self and cultivate humility and contemplation. To
this end, *Murphy* quotes Geulincx's most well-known adage: 'ubi nihil vales,
ibi nihil velis' (where you're worth nothing you should desire nothing) (124).
Its hero fastidiously strives to leave the external world of bodies and seeks to
empty himself of the desire for worldly things. Such ascetic principles are
to be found in Beckett's early work in various forms and influenced by a
variety of thinkers. For instance, Schopenhauer advocates, as an antidote to
the suffering of life, the suppression of human yearning, rather than any
attempt to satiate it. Satisfying desire only gives temporary relief; instead one
ought to try to withdraw from the faculty of human desire altogether
by living a contemplative, ascetic life. Beckett approvingly alludes to this

philosophy in *Proust*, when he speaks of the 'wisdom that consists not in the satisfaction but in the ablation of desire' (P 18).

Yet, in the long run, Murphy violates the ethics of Geulincx precisely by desiring something after his death, by writing a will. His death is caused by someone pulling the wrong chain in the lavatory and turning on the gas in Murphy's bedroom, which is ignited by his lit candle. Murphy, lashed tight to his rocking-chair, burns to death. In death Murphy's aspirations are as eccentric and unconventional as in life. His written will requests that his body be cremated and his ashes flushed down the lavatory in the Abbey Theatre in Dublin, preferably during a performance. His wishes after his death are as thwarted as his ambitions for pure self-containment in life. The man entrusted with the duty of carrying his ashes to the Abbey gets drunk in a public house, where the ashes end up 'freely distributed over the floor of the saloon; and before another dayspring greyened the earth had been swept away with the sand, the beer, the butts, the glass, the matches, the spits, the vomit' (187). Murphy's grand intellectual and spiritual enterprise, his effort to transcend the body, to purify himself of the debasements of corporeal desire, end mixed in bar-room filth. The wisdom that consists not in the satisfaction but in the ablation of desire, of which he wrote approvingly in *Proust*, is rather mocked in *Murphy*. The thwarting of his written will is, in one sense, a deserved punishment. In death Murphy breaks his own ascetic resolutions, his own urge to abnegate worldly desires and pursuits. Leaving a 'will' at all indicates an act of yearning at odds with his intellectual outlook. However, even more fundamentally, Murphy is caught up in a self-defeating enterprise. His ascetic impulses generate their own undoing. Surely to desire the extinction of desire is an enterprise which, since it creates that which it wants to extinguish, is an enterprise which must end in failure. 'It is useless not to seek, not to want,' the narrator of Beckett's next novel, *Watt*, reflects,

> for when you cease to seek you start to find, and when you cease to want, then life begins to ram her fish and chips down your gullet until you puke, and then the puke down your gullet until you puke the puke, and then the puked puke until you begin to like it.   (43)

Watt

Famous for its endless lists of descriptive permutations, *Watt* is much more formally audacious than *Murphy*. It too is full of predetermined sequences and closed systems, but it complicates the realist structure far more radically

than its predecessor. To begin with, the text thumbs its nose at the very idea
of a completed novel. In certain respects, it looks like a mere draft. For
instance, there are a number of question marks floating around the text
without apparent reason, like personal notes to a hypothetical author that a
particular passage or sentence is in need of revision, correction or comple-
tion. At the end of the novel, in the notorious 'Addenda', are several dislocated lines and passages which we are advised in a footnote 'should be
carefully studied' because only 'fatigue and disgust' prevent their incorporation' (247). The text clearly flaunts the idea that it is unfinished, hence
revealing something of the process of novel-writing as well as simply deliver-
ing the finished product, with all its rough edges carefully planed smooth. Of
course, Beckett did not really abandon the text at its penultimate draft. The
text is merely deploying the illusion of incompletion in order to kick against
what Beckett regarded as the calcified, delusory conventions of slice-of-life
realism. 'To read Balzac', claims the narrator of *Dream of Fair to Middling
Women*,

> is to receive the impression of a chloroformed world. He is absolute
> master of his material, he can do what he likes with it, he can foresee
> and calculate its least vicissitude, he can write the end of his book before
> he has finished the first paragraph, because he has turned all his
> creatures into clockwork cabbages and can rely on their staying put
> wherever needed or staying going at whatever speed in whatever
> direction he chooses.[3]

Beckett is clearly setting his teeth against the 'chloroformed world' of the
great nineteenth-century realist by breaking apart the sense of continuity and
control.

To this end, the text ruptures the linear narrative with which it begins. It is
as if it cannot make up its mind which story to tell. The opening of the novel,
with its simple third-person narrative treatment of Mr Hackett, might make a
reader reasonably expect that he and Mr and Mrs Nixon, with whom he has a
conversation, will be the subjects of the story or will at least have some role to
play in the plot. Certainly a traditional novel which spends so long on these
characters would surely develop them or bring them back into the story in
some way. But this novel almost seems to tire of them with the appearance of
Watt and, with this eponymous hero, leaves the bourgeois world of propriety
and respectability and enters the strange and estranging world of Mr Knott's
house. Belacqua and Murphy may have some peculiar ideas, but, by and
large, we experience the world in a similar way to them. The same could not
be said about Watt.

Another feature of the narrative which flaunts its own textual and constructed nature is the seepage between the supposed mind of the characters, particularly Watt, and the language of the narrator. For the narrator and Watt, though clearly distinct, share a mania for explanation, for logical procedures dislodged from any recognisable point, for endlessly articulated combinations of possibilities. So, when he meets Mr Spiro on the train, the narrator tells us how Watt hears voices in his head which either sing, cry, state or murmur, then proceeds to list all possible partial and full combinations of these four sounds and utterances. The narrator, in an anticipation of the obsessive permutations which lie in store later in the text, lists them all (27). Why the need for this exhaustive inventory? This is a question that many readers of the novel have asked. Watt's mental habits are described in Part 2. He has an obsessive need to think through all possibilities and combinations of possibilities for the routines and structures around him. Hence, for instance, we get Watt's full consideration of the problem of the disposal of Mr Knott's food in pages and pages of grimly methodical listing. The point is that the narrator performs on Watt the same procedure of descriptive permutation that Watt does on the objects and experiences he encounters. So the narrator's mind is rather like Watt's. Is this to say that Watt might actually *be* the narrator? If anyone in the novel takes on that role it is Sam, whom we meet in Part 3. Far from Watt being the narrator, the blurring between the voices highlights the textual, linguistic nature of Watt's psychology. The narrative is not 'really' given by Watt – rather Watt is given by the narrative. Like all characters in Beckett's novels, he is simply a textual function, a product of language, as opposed to the supposedly 'rounded', fully developed character of the realist novel. By blurring the distinction between the third-person narrative voice and that of the character in this way, the text demonstrates the porous nature of selfhood and the illusory idea of the fully rounded narrative 'character'. This is another way in which this text unsettles the assumptions and conventions of the realist novel.

The sheer ludicrousness of life in Mr Knott's house and in the asylum of Part 3, the bizarrely regulated routines and rituals, also highlight that this is a textual world. It is clearly not aimed at convincing the reader of its slice-of-life plausibility. This is not to say that it does not strive to access a deeper truth, to bear witness in its perplexed forms to a layer of experience inaccessible to more conventional fiction. *Watt* and the novels which follow, while showing aspects of the world that are recognisable, will also show aspects that are surreal, nonsensical and bizarre. The point here and later is to puncture the artifice of fiction, by depicting something preposterous – the house of Mr Knott, with his clockwork routines, his continual changes in shape and physical appearance, his strictly regulated sequence of small, fat, shabby, seedy, juicy, bandy-legged, pot-bellied, pot-bottomed servants and big, bony, seedy, shabby, haggard, knock-kneed, rotten-toothed, red-nosed servants. The story of Watt's stay in Mr Knott's house and his subsequent residence in what appears to be a mental asylum of some sort are richly weird and wayward. That these elements are preceded by the story of Mr Hackett and the railway station indicates a departure both literal (Watt getting on to the train) and figurative (the move away from plausible fiction). Watt, and the narrative which tells his tale, both leave the ordinary and the realistic world, the world of characters like Mr Hackett and the denizens of the railway station, with all its parodied notions of propriety, its dreary gossip and formulaic exchanges.

Watt, then, far exceeds the oddity of *Murphy*, which, for all the eccentricity of its characters, falls short of the fantastic or absurd. The style and tone of the later novel, however, is calmer and less heavy with erudition. But beneath the straightforward and direct, if often exhaustive and pointless, narrative momentum lies a radical perplexity. The novel plays off oppositions between order and disorder. The methods of description, where all possibilities are exhaustively listed, may seem bizarre, but in another sense they signal a mania for order, for covering every possibility, for obsessive narrative control of events. But at the same time as an iron descriptive discipline is exerted (no possibility can be allowed to slip through the narrative net), the reader will be forgiven for experiencing bewilderment as to the purpose and point of the various activities that take place. Why does Watt go to Mr Knott's house? Why do there always have to be two servants? 'Pervasive as ozone, uncertainty invests the pores and interstices of the narrative,' Hugh Kenner remarks.[4] It is as if narrative control, including all the manically inclusive descriptions, is a compensatory strategy for the lack of clarity in how to explain or understand events.

In other words, if the world is indecipherable, and Watt seems to find it so, then the prospects for mimesis or representation become pretty dismal. At its most basic level *Watt* is a desperate parody of the futility of representation. More particularly, the text raises questions about the possibility of the objective record in any context. Often in fiction, third-person narrative purports a degree of 'impartiality', or disinterest, as if we are being told a story for the purposes of reportage. In other words, third-person narrative tends to occlude selectivity, or value judgements, in the same way as a reporter will aspire to tell the 'full story'. But telling the full story in *Watt*, reaching for the impartial or unselective narrative stance, is pushed to its ludicrous extreme. If the descriptive technique strives to be neutral and objective, it also aims to be complete, to leave nothing out ('What not' is one echo of 'Watt Knott'). The long lists, the repetitions, the covering of every potential is, in a sense, a scrupulous concern not to leave anything out, to give a full and complete rendering of the story. The attempt is ultimately grotesque and ridiculous. The permutations and possibilities throng into tedium and become impossible to read. One reason, then, why objective representation is impossible is because engagements with the world cannot be separated from value judgements – some things need to be left out.

Language here is often fundamentally mismatched with what it seeks to articulate, the perceiver disconnected from the perceived. Again and again, there are slippages and dud notes in the attempts at verisimilitude. The random question marks peppered throughout the text read like inexplicable viruses in a computer printout. Arsene is eager to point out to Watt that his narrative is unreliable because 'what we know partakes in no small measure of the nature of what has so happily been called the unutterable or ineffable, so that any attempt to utter or eff it is doomed to fail, doomed, doomed to fail' (61). Famously, Watt is thwarted in his effort to name the pot that was not a pot. This moment indicates the elusiveness of the named object, its resistance to the efforts of language to pin it down: 'it was just this hair-breadth departure from the nature of a true pot that so excruciated Watt' (78). He wouldn't have minded, we are told, if the approximation had been less close. Then he could have acknowledged that the pot was indefinable and the finality would have provided him with the 'semantic succour' (79) that he so desperately craves: 'For then he would not have said, This is a pot, and yet not a pot, no, but then he would have said, This is something of which I do not know the name' (78).

Naming things, for Watt, is an effort to control them, to freeze them into safe conceptual categories. He needs the certainty of being either the controller or the controlled, a subject or an object. Being a servant, having his days organised around routine and repetition, allows him certainty amidst the confusion and change. If Watt is unable to define, then he is content to be defined – and this is another of his attractions to a role in Mr Knott's establishment. Mr Hackett and the Nixons consider the reasons why Watt left the tram before it arrived at the train station: 'Too fearful to assume himself the onus of a decision, said Mr Hackett, he refers it to the frigid machinery of a time-space relation' (19). This is what the existentialists might call 'bad faith' or 'inauthenticity': avoiding the burdensome reality of sheer freedom and loneliness by taking on a pre-defined role or looking to bogus external certainties to give one's life order and purpose. Perhaps this is the motivation behind Watt's employment in the house of Mr Knott. Arsene

whatever the narrators' perplexity, and however repetitious and bewildered the language that registers it, the prose is at the same time enduringly calm and serene. In the early works the third-person narrative voice was cluttered with erudition, the sentences were weighty and arcane. Though not without allusion to other texts, the learning in the trilogy is much more lubricated into the narrative flow, and its language as a result is smoother and more tranquil. It moves easily and without strain and is, at many moments, beautiful and evocative.

Throughout the narrative, the language has this sort of understated seren-ity – cadenced sentences, rhythmically composed and hinged around care-fully crafted clauses. If the material is chaotic, messy and disjointed – like the rambling, fragmented stories of his narrators – then their plight is rendered with painstaking, almost balletic exactitude. This may be one reason why Beckett claimed in an interview that in his work form and content remain separate. That, unlike Kafka, there is 'consternation' behind the form, not in it: 'Kafka's form is classic, it goes on like a steam roller – almost serene. It seems to be threatened all the time – but the consternation is in the form. In my work there is consternation behind the form, not in the form.'[5] As a young man, Beckett praised Joyce's 'Work in Progress' (the precursor of *Finnegans Wake*) for a subversive identification of form and content: 'Here form *is* content, content *is* form' (D 27). One of the ways in which his own post-war work reacts against the methods of Joyce is in his scrupulous exploration of that area where content and form, the mess and the way it is described, are distinct. The turmoil in the minds of his narrators is typically transmitted in an unwavering, steady-handed, quiet prose, strikingly at peace with itself.

The confusion and uncertainty underneath this serene, pared-back prose is, importantly, not confined to the characters themselves. Just as the speakers often bemoan the inscrutability of the forces which compel them, so too the reader is denied the reassuring presence of purposes or 'goals'. If Moran is not fully sure why he is pursuing Molloy, what the reasons are for Youdi to be issuing his reports, then this information is also withheld from us. In this respect, the text does not just *express* bewilderment and confusion, it *enacts* it. If we feel bereft of meaning or rationality in encountering these novels, then it is perhaps worth bearing in mind that this 'absence' may actually be part of the text's function.

If this is so, then bringing clarity to our reading, explaining its 'meaning' or decoding its complexities may be, paradoxically, to mangle and misrepre-sent. If the point of a novel, its aesthetic effect as it were, is to withhold clarity of theme or rational 'message', then explaining that novel, translating it into coherent themes, is in a sense to lose it. Critical approaches to the trilogy are thrown back on themselves: 'reading' the trilogy immediately asks questions about how the trilogy should be read in so far as it challenges many of the procedures and conventions underlying critical interpretation. As ever, we need to proceed with caution, and with proper critical circumspection. An attentive encounter with Beckett's fiction is one which is alert to the quality and nature of the voices, the structure of the story, how the narrative is being told as much as what it 'means'. There is little point in pillaging these texts for readily packaged themes or clear messages, no point in seeking to iron out their dislocations and difficulties. On the other hand, we cannot simply ignore the challenge to interpretation that these elusive texts pose, eschewing their ambiguities and perplexities for the appreciation of a nicely caught cadence. Even if we fumble the questions, it might not be a bad starting point to try to identify what some of them are.

Molloy

For whom does Molloy write? He tells us at the start of the novel (which is also the end of the novel, as it seems the ensuing story is told retrospectively) that a man comes and collects his pages and gives him money. Are the people this man represents the same people for whom Moran works, namely the mysterious Youdi and his messenger, Gaber? Why do the quests of both men, Molloy to find his mother, Moran to find Molloy, seemingly end unsuccessfully, with Molloy in a ditch and Moran returning home without having found Molloy? Or are they unsuccessful? Molloy begins writing his story from his mother's room, so it seems he eventually gets there. Moran, even if he does not find Molloy as a separate individual, in one sense turns into his quarry, in that he increasingly resembles Molloy by the end of his story. Is becoming someone equivalent to finding him? Molloy also declares that he resembles his mother more and more. Is this because he too has become that which he sought?

More local questions about the novel gather too. Why does Molloy go through his celebrated routine with his sucking stones? Why is Moran fascinated by the dance of his bees? Why does Molloy's narrative begin with an encounter in the mountains between two men, A and C, who do not turn up in the narrative again? What is the significance of the silver, sawhorse-like object (a knife-rest, if Malone is to be believed) he takes from Lousse's house? Why does Molloy kick the charcoal burner to death? Should we think of this killing, when we later read that Moran also bludgeons a stranger to death? Are these murders to be read as connected to the physical changes that both these men undergo?

To these questions we could add many others. One certainty that emerges from this novel is that certainty is in desperately short supply. This will be a fundamental theme of Beckett's work from now on. The gratifying certainty of clear themes or stances will be denied readers or spectators. The dangers are still in the neatness of identification. But, just as in *Waiting for Godot*, we are tantalised with hints, clues, suggestions and implicit invitations to find significance which are then withdrawn. In *Molloy*, one such invitation bears on the figure of the 'mother':

> And if ever I'm reduced to looking for a meaning in my life, you never can tell, it's in that old mess I'll stick my nose to begin with, the mess of that poor old uniparous whore and myself the last of my foul brood, neither man nor beast.   (19)

Given that he would go in search of his mother when 'reduced' to looking for meaning casts a particular light on the actual physical search for his mother that he undertakes. It encourages us to read this search in excess of its literal significance. Yet our attempt to read it in symbolic or grandly existentialist terms is undermined by the mordantly dismissive and contemptuous view he holds of his mother ('the mess of that poor old uniparous whore'). His general attitude to her is shockingly, but also hilariously, black and bleak, as when, in his efforts to extract money, he tries to communicate with her by knocking on her head. As so often with birth and generation in Beckett's world, filial gratitude tends to be as rare as Hamm's painkillers.

Nonetheless, amidst the mess, the squalidness, the corporeality, the scatology, the gleeful subversions of social nicety, there are a lot of rich and resonant motifs and preoccupations, however shorn of ostensible purpose and plot. Take, for instance, the quest model. Both parts of this novel involve a quest story, Molloy's for his mother, Moran's for Molloy. The idea of the quest is one of the oldest and most pervasive plot structures in world literature, never more so, one might add, than when (as with Homer's *Odyssey*, to which there are many allusions in *Molloy*) the quest is for 'Home'. Even if Molloy is not searching for his literal home, one of the many ramifications of the search for the 'mother' is the idea of *origin* of some kind. After all, it is from his mother, as Molloy mournfully remembers, whence he came: 'What a rest to speak of bicycles and horns. Unfortunately it is not of them I have to speak, but of her who brought me into the world, through the hole in her arse if my memory is correct. First taste of the shit' (17). If going home is a 'return' in spatial or geographical terms, then going to the mother is such in temporal or historical terms. The start of the novel, when Molloy indicates that he is writing his story from his mother's room, indicates that he may have succeeded in the quest, though that he is on his own, that he has 'taken her place', suggests a refusal of external authority, of inherited notions of identity. This is only one of the many respects in which the quest model is deployed and subsequently subverted and dismantled. Each protagonist of *Molloy* starts by searching for someone else, but ends by returning to himself, or to a different (perhaps deeper) version of himself.

We could point at other motifs in the novel which reinforce this theme of return. Getting old is itself a return of sorts, and often involves a repeat of the behaviour of childhood. Beckett's geriatric characters have much in common with the very young, as well as the very old. Moran, it seems, ends his journey in a state of babyish incontinence, and there is something childlike in the oral gratification that Molloy obtains from sucking his stones. If there is a movement back to the mother, back to childhood (with all its attendant helplessness), then there is also the suggestion of a sort of species regression. After all, Molloy ends up in the forest (from whence the human species emerged), crawling 'on his belly, like a reptile' (83). It is as if he goes through evolution in reverse. As Molloy says of his mother, 'Ah the old bitch, a nice dose she gave me, she and her lousy unconquerable genes' (75). Perhaps another ramification of Molloy's search for his mother is the return of species to its origins, the reversing of evolution.

So, for all its seeming opacity and perplexity, *Molloy* points towards some basic and fundamental themes. If the plot, such as it is, incorporates the 'quest' motif and the search for the 'mother' and origins, it treats, however inaccessibly, some other large topics along the way: love, death, memory, crime, guilt, murder, family, work, authority, rural versus urban life, politics, sexuality and disease, to mention just a few. If this is a peripatetic novel based around a journey, it also incorporates a bourgeois comedy (in Moran's relations with his son), a detective novel, a romance. So it is a text which beckons towards the profound and elemental, even as it deflates any attempt at portentousness. In its deployment of the quest for selfhood and origin, it keys into the fundamental tropes, at the same time as mocking any possibility that such assured principles can be known or articulated.

The process of physical change in both protagonists is presented at certain moments as a shedding of protective layers. As Moran puts it, 'And I seemed to see myself ageing as swiftly as a day-fly. But the idea of ageing was not exactly the one which offered itself to me. And what I saw was more like a crumbling, a frenzied collapsing of all that had always protected me from all I was condemned to be' (136–7). So the loss of the body is a sort of collapse of the battlements, a revelation of a vulnerable self underneath his role as strict father and respected citizen. Not surprisingly in a novel so wholly disdainful of the body, so scornfully alert to its weaknesses, illness, old age, degeneration and decay, the body can be relied upon to be unreliable. But there is at the same time, a sense of ambivalence about who is abandoning what. Is the body letting Moran down or is he, on some ineffable level, repudiating the body in order to access some more authentic interior self?

In general, religion of any institutional sort is given short shrift in the trilogy. Moran's Catholicism is witheringly portrayed at the start of his narrative, while his supposed pilgrimage to see the 'Turdy Madonna' revisits the early conflation of maternity and excrement in Molloy's mind. Later on, after his condition has much deteriorated, 'certain questions of a theological nature' preoccupy Moran, but the list he contrives is a dark, quasi-blasphemous parody of the doctrinal catechism: '1. What value is to be attached to the theory that Eve sprang, not from Adam's rib, but from a tumour in the fat of his leg (arse?)?' (153); '14. Might not the beatific vision become a source of boredom, in the long run?' (154). However, even though the profane may be the opposite of the sacred, they both deploy the same vocabulary and structures of thought. The conventional language of faith may be scorned here but it is still significant that Moran turns to this religious, albeit impious, language at the peak of his dereliction. Similarly Molloy, as his bodily pain and debilitation increases, regards his plight as a sort of *via dolorosa*. The progress he makes, however slow and painful it has always been, was now 'changed, saving your presence, to a veritable calvary, with no limit to its stations and no hope of crucifixion, though I say it myself, and no Simon, and reduced me to frequent halts' (72). There is a sense that, like in *Waiting for Godot*, a religious context is evoked even as redemption or salvation is withheld, just as Molloy cannot hope to even achieve crucifixion at the end of his 'calvary' (a word used to describe the route of Christ's Passion), let alone resurrection.

That said, despite the suffering of the characters and the seeming repudiation of conventional religious redemption, there are some moments that evoke spiritual advancement or insight, particularly as the characters' physical depletion advances. One is when Molloy leaves the forest at the end of his story and, hearing birdsong, realises that 'Molloy could stay, where he happened to be' (84). Birdsong has quasi-mystical overtones, and the rest and stasis that Molloy earns after his long quest beckon, mysteriously, towards a sort of atonement. Another occurs during Moran's narrative, in a moment much more rarefied than the clunky religious philosophy he so ineptly seeks to articulate. Immediately after his contemplations of his own bodily decay, he seeks to describe the changes in his own mental processes 'so changed from what I was' (136). In order to articulate his experience, he recounts a vision of a face, suffused with light and serenity:

> it was like a kind of clawing towards a light and countenance I could not
> name, that I had once known and long denied. But what words can
> describe this sensation at first all darkness and bulk, with a noise like the
> grinding of stones, then suddenly as soft as water flowing. And then
> I saw a little globe swaying up slowly from the depths, through the quiet
> water, smooth at first, and scarcely paler than its escorting ripples, then
> little by little a face, with holes for the eyes and mouth and other
> wounds, and nothing to show if it was a man's face or a woman's face, a
> young face or an old face, or if its calm too was not an effect of the water
> trembling between it and the light.   (137)

This vivid description of a luminous face emerging from the water is certainly beautiful and perhaps beatific. The soft sounds of the water and the
calmness of the light come as a relief after the darkness and the grinding of
rock. It is a birth of sorts: a less defined and confined identity rising from the
ruination of the personality that he has shed. It has the feel of breaking
carapace ('the frenzied collapsing of all that had always protected me from all
I was condemned to be'). He goes on to speak of his 'growing resignation of
being dispossessed of self' (137). This dispossession, as already said, is often
regarded as a sort of distillation, a movement towards ever purer forms of
subjectivity. Descent into disability is, in the logic of *Molloy*, counterpointed
by a sort of ascent or elevation of the mind or soul, just as Murphy had to tie
himself up in his search for mental freedom. The ascent of the featureless face
from the rippling water could be a metaphor for this opposition. In Moran's
case, the subsequent killing of the man with a face which 'vaguely resembled
my own' reinforces the sense of a new selfhood, in revolt against its own
previous incarnation.

These narrators are continually answerable to edicts and instructions,
authority figures of one sort or another. The immersive impression that the
trilogy imparts, that of a movement inwards or downwards, is also brought
home by the shift in the positioning of authority. At the start of Part 2,
Moran's relationships with authority figures are clearly demarcated. He is an
agent who receives orders from Youdi via his messenger Gaber. The system of
agents, secrets, intermediaries, mysterious orders and missions and edicts
from above has led some to find in these figures the traces of fascism and the
Second World War. Others have seen a religious dimension here, pointing
out that Youdi is almost an anagram for the French word 'Dieu' (God) while
his messenger, Gaber, evokes the archangel Gabriel. For centuries monarchs
and human leaders have justified themselves with divine authority – their
rule on earth, mandated by God, replicating his rule in heaven. Beckett
inverts this model. Rather than human hierarchy taking on the supposed

attributes of the divine, Beckett's work often reveals a God-like figure adopting the menace of secular human domination.

Sometimes encounters with authority figures generate the comic incomprehension of the Beckettian vagrant confronting the forces of conventional society. Such is certainly the case of Molloy's encounter with the (clearly Irish) police force early in his narrative. As the stories and the trilogy progress, however, the sources of power cease to be recognisably worldly and become less parodied and more internal. By the time Molloy gets to the forest, the imperatives he must follow are those he hears in his head. Again the voices of authority become internal voices when the physical powers diminish:

> But I could not, stay in the forest I mean, I was not free to. That is to say I could have, physically nothing could have been easier, but I was not purely physical, I lacked something, and I would have had the feeling, if I had stayed in the forest, of going against an imperative, as least I had that impression. (79)

His bodily deterioration makes him no longer 'purely physical' and this redirects the authority to which he is subject onto internal voices, which he calls his 'prompters'. The imperatives he feels are strongly linked to his committing a fault, to a sense of 'sin': 'For I have greatly sinned, at all times, greatly sinned against my prompters' (79). Nonetheless, if subject to instructions, Molloy is still denied a clear goal or destination. Just as the two parts of this novel chronicle an unravelling of physical selfhood, so too they meander away from the goal that they initially pursue – Molloy for his mother, Moran for Molloy. And the imperatives that Molloy hears re-enact this wavering, this hesitancy. They 'nearly all bore on the same question', that of his relations with his mother, but, having set him in motion, 'they began to falter, then went silent, leaving me there like a fool who neither knows where he is going nor why he is going there' (80). The goal or the end of both narrative quests unravels before our eyes, like a metaphor for the abandonment of the principles of story-telling itself.

For all his innocence and bewilderment, Molloy continually ponders what it is to say or to know. The language describes and narrates. But, crucially, it often reflects on what it means to describe and narrate, and these reflections exacerbate his unease. He is continually worried that he gets it wrong, that his memory is faulty, or that his will, desires or mere consciousness muddle up the processes of tale-telling. In his earlier writing Beckett considers how voluntary memory distorts the recollected object because of the accretions of hindsight – things become different through retrospect so that choosing to remember is always misremembering. Only through involuntary memory, when a recollection rushes back unbidden, does one get close to the actuality of lost time. Similarly, Molloy wants to take himself out of the narrative process, to let his story be told without actually willing it. Like a child bursting to tell a story, the wilful story-teller is always over-anxious. Molloy aspires to repress his own will or voice in order the better to tell the truth:

> Not to want to say, not to know what you want to say, not to be able to say what you think you want to say, and never to stop saying, or hardly ever, that is the thing to keep in mind, even in the heat of composition. (27)

This seems a bit rich for a narrative so preoccupied with subjectivity, so intensely geared to the first person, so attentive to consciousness and its processes. It could be, however, that Molloy strives to prevent conscious will from mangling the veracity of the story he wants to tell, just as conscious or voluntary memory bears false witness to the past. Significantly, there may be a connection between this urge to tell the story without the distortions of wanting to tell it and the opposition, already discussed above, between serene language and chaotic content in the trilogy as whole. The impartial sayer (the 'incurious seeker') may be the equivalent of a literary style or a form that keeps its distance, in terms of structure and pattern, from the torment it is describing.

Molloy comes to see the opacity of his life and surroundings as helping him achieve the higher, quasi-spiritual peace that comes from contemplation,

> For to know nothing is nothing, not to want to know anything likewise, but to be beyond knowing anything, to know you are beyond knowing anything, that is when peace enters in, to the soul of the incurious seeker. (59)

Much as he strives for this peace, he cannot help his frustrations at the inadequacies of language. Like so many of the earlier Beckett characters, he cannot seem to find the quietism he seeks. Words are too unhappily distant from their referents. Just as that ineffable pot could not be properly signified by the word 'pot' in *Watt*, so too does language here seem distant from that which it purports to signify. Earlier Molloy has expressed his great dissatisfactions with the mismatch between words and what they strive to articulate:

> And even my sense of identity was wrapped in a namelessness often hard to penetrate, as we have just seen I think. And so on for all the other things that made merry with my senses. Yes, even then, when

already all was fading, waves and particles, there could be no things
but nameless things, no names but thingless names. I say that now,
but after all what do I know now about then, now when the icy words
hail down upon me, the icy meanings, and the world dies too, foully
named. All I know is what the words know, and the dead things, and
that makes a handsome little sum, with a beginning middle and an end
as in the well-built phrase and the long sonata of the dead.   (30–1)

This passage merits some consideration. In it one can unpack the ambivalence at the root of the debate in Beckett criticism as to whether he should
be regarded as a late modernist or an early postmodernist. On the one hand,
'nameless things' implies the inadequacy of language, its tendency to distort
and misrepresent the world, to impose its false coherence and clarity onto
that which it strives to represent. One could draw a comparison here with
the modernist experimentation of the early decades of the twentieth century
in which there was a perception that received literary and linguistic forms
needed renovation in order the better to express a reality that seemed
resistant to articulation. On the other hand, 'thingless names' emphasises
instead the *constitutive* power of language. The reality which is being
articulated should not be considered in any sense anterior to, or separable
from, the language which is expressing it. The language gives the world its
being, it does not reflect it. This could be called the 'postmodern' perspective, in which language or signs evoke or create the world. They do not
simply name or articulate it. Is Beckett a late modernist, striving to find new
forms to articulate the endlessly opaque and recalcitrant world, or an early
postmodernist, registering that language, culture, names, do not simply
label or express something, but rather construct that something themselves?

The final sentence of the passage seems to withdraw from the two positions, expressing the ignorance of the narrator ('what do I know now about
then') and blaming the words and meanings that fall like ice, freezing the
fluidity of the self and the world ('the world dies too, foully named').

Malone Dies

Malone is relieved to anticipate that when he dies 'it will be all over with the
Murphys, Merciers, Molloys, Morans, Malones, unless it goes on beyond the
grave' (217). Since he is both protagonist and story-teller, the implication is
that he is also the creator of these other characters. 'How many have I killed,'
he wonders, 'hitting them on the head or setting fire to them?', alluding to the
man Moran bludgeoned and to Murphy's untimely end. Significantly, he also
includes his own name, Malone, in the list. He is both the inventor of

characters, but also one of them, simultaneously subject and object, controller and controlled.

But then, as Beckett's work often implies, there is a sense in which self-consciousness or self-description is always a form of self-splitting. To be self-aware is to consider oneself, however implicitly, from an external point of view. To act spontaneously in the world, to have sensations and appetites like a baby or an animal, is one thing, but to be aware of oneself as a thinking, appetitive individual is consciousness of a different order. The self becomes both a perceiver and a perceived. The old Cartesian dictum 'I think therefore I am' is in a sense a division of the self into two: a self that does the thinking and the self that perceives the self that is thinking. Once the 'I' can be aware of the 'I' then there are in one sense two 'I's: a subject that is aware and an object of that awareness. But, if so, then the perceiving self, the subject, could itself become an object of perception. Just as I could think about myself thinking, so too could I think about the 'self' that is thinking about myself thinking. In theory, this splitting could escalate until the subject becomes a series of Russian dolls. A comparable metaphor of selfhood could, again, be an onion. In the trilogy, the layers are peeled away to get to an ever-elusive pith or essence, where the elemental rent of subjectivity is healed and where the self is simultaneously perceiver and perceived, subject and object.

Beckett's characters, as already seen, often seek to escape from an excess of self-consciousness. They refuse, typically, too much philosophical or abstract reflection on the condition they inhabit, disdaining like Malone 'all this ballsaching poppycock about life and death' (206). In both prose and drama they often seek absorption in a game or in a story rather than the stricken awareness of who or where they are. From the beginning, the ailing Malone seeks a 'natural', that is an unreflective, death:

> Yes I shall be natural at last, I shall suffer more, then less, without drawing any conclusions, I shall pay less heed to myself, I shall be neither hot nor cold any more, I shall be tepid, I shall die tepid, without enthusiasm.
> I shall not watch myself die, that would spoil everything.   (165)

He chooses not to watch himself die at this crucial moment, not to bifurcate himself into perceiver and perceived. In other words, striving for an integration of the self as consciousness ebbs, he aims to keep 'self'-consciousness at bay. The way he sets out to achieve this is by deploying a careful sequence of strategic distractions: telling himself four (adjusted to three) stories, performing an inventory of his possessions, and finally dying. It does not quite work out like this. The sequence gets disrupted and disfigured by the constant self-interruptions of his stories and expressions of disgust about how bad they are – 'What tedium', 'This is awful'. His inventory is half-inserted as asides during the narrative, not listed methodically towards the end as he had planned. At the moment of death, however, it *does* seem he avoids watching himself expire, for his story of Lemuel continues as he dies. In the last few lines, as the last characters in Malone's story are violently dispatched, his narrative voice begins to flail and fail, the language breaks down into separate words, and partial lines, indicating both the dying narrative and the dying narrator. It is one of the few moments in Beckett's oeuvre where form mimics content so explicitly.

While *Molloy*, with its interest in motherhood and physical regression, probed origins and archetypes, *Malone Dies* probes endings and dismemberment. The two sections of *Molloy* come sequentially; *Malone Dies* operates within a frame narrative: Malone alone in his room and his story about Sapo/Macmann are interspersed and alternating. Both parts of *Molloy* tend towards movement. The two levels of *Malone Dies* tend towards fixity and stasis: Malone stays in his room; Sapo, a brooding child, sits in the Lambert's house. Macmann lies cruciform in the rain for long periods and finally ends up in an institution resembling that where Malone is now.

These distinctions between the two novels, however, are only provisional. Macmann may be still for a lot of his life but he moves a great deal in the final pages of his story, just as Molloy comes to a definite stasis at the end of his. Moreover the poles between origins and ends – mother's room/womb in *Molloy* and the deathbed in *Malone Dies* – are as much doubles as opposites. If Malone is dying, he is also being born, 'far already from the world that parts its labia and lets me go' (174). Repeatedly in the novel, in a very familiar Beckettian trope, death is configured as a form of birth, final throes and initial pangs brought into explicit alignment. Near the end, Malone remarks that 'The ceiling rises and falls, rises and falls, rhythmically, as when I was a foetus' (259–60).

Molloy and *Malone Dies* were planned as companion novels (the idea for *The Unnamable* followed later) and they have many shared characteristics as well as contrasts. Malone is 'simply what I am called now', and he has many recollections of forest, bicycle, bell, crutch, ambulance, sucking stones, hat-tied-to-chin-by-string, all of which refer back to Molloy/Moran. Recollections, however, are unreliable in the trilogy. He does not remember how he got into the room he is now in and, though his stories are mere 'play', mere invented distractions, they become hopelessly mingled with details from his own past: 'What tedium. And I call that playing. I wonder if I am not talking yet again about myself. Shall I be incapable, to the end, of lying on any other subject?' (174). He makes a mess of the sequence leading into his death, as might have been predicted. This is partly because he is afraid of this mingling, afraid that the stories might be about himself. 'I must simply be on my guard, reflecting on what I have said before I go on and stopping, each time disaster threatens, to look at myself as I am. That is just what I wanted to avoid' (174). He wants to avoid looking at himself because, as already seen, he does not want to die in a 'self-conscious' manner. But it is hard for him to keep away this self-reflection, hard for him to keep himself out of his stories. This is what causes the alternating, rather jumpy narrative changes between his narrative and his present condition. The switches are signalled, for the most part, by a new paragraph, a shift from third-person to first-person narrative. The narrative flow, therefore, is far less serene than that of *Molloy*, despite Malone's early determination to make his stories 'calm' and 'almost lifeless, like the teller' (165).

Malone's stories are intensely coloured not just by his own past, his own life-story, but also seemingly by his present. The most obvious example is the killing spree at the end of the novel: the creatures in his stories get killed off just as, presumably, a higher authority is killing him. But there are other examples of this bleeding across narrative levels throughout the text. Malone's obsession with material things, for instance, is replicated in that of the Saposcat parents with their fixation about the gift of a pen they plan to give their son. Again, as with Moran's relationship with his son, we have a parody of bourgeois parental solicitude and ambition in this family scene. The conventionality of the Saposcats' ambitions is offset by the darkness of the surrounding tale, the brooding melancholia of their dolt-like son. While there is violence and killing in both parts of *Molloy*, the brutality in this novel is even greater. Sapo (the name by which young Saposcat is at first known) makes trips to the Lambert farm, where he sits silently amidst the squalid and humdrum slaughter and death. 'Lambert' is a distinctly Irish Catholic name, and these passages are haunted by caste and class interactions. 'The inadequacy of the exchanges between rural and urban areas had not escaped the excellent youth,' remarks the narrator with ironic brio (180). 'Big Lambert' is a pig-slaughterer, a job he performs with much relish, and the violence of his job spills into his relations with his wife and family. While the narrative proffers some beautiful descriptions of nature, Sapo is 'blind to its beauty, and to its utility, and to the little wild many-coloured flowers happy among the crops and weeds' (189). The pastoral delicacy is repeatedly overhauled by violence, death and pitilessness. So, for instance, we have the story of the death and burial of the worn-out mule that Old Lambert purchased outside the slaughter-house two years before. As so often in

Beckett, dark humour comes from parody and anomalous juxtaposition. The story of Lambert's farm conjoins moral and familial propriety with casual cruelty and degradation.

A comparable sort of mordant humour comes from the sexual relationship later in the novel between Macmann and Moll. Just like that between Lousse and Molloy in the earlier novel, the conventions of romantic love are mercilessly sent up first by the physical grotesqueness of the lovers and subsequently by the distinctly unheroic manner in which the lovers part. Her maudlin letters to him, and his incompetent ditties to her in response, are hilarious parody of the language of romantic love and its various clichéd poses. Despite the predictions of the two, and their advanced age, the relationship does not end poignantly in the grave, but rather with the waning of Moll's love, following the rise of Macmann's. For all the pretensions of self-sacrifice here, sexual love is as caught up in a system of exchange, of 'the quantum of wantum', as it was in *Murphy*.

Even when their love is at its most intense, however, it never surpasses Moll's feelings of duty to her job in the institution in which Macmann is held. This betrays their love for the comical charade it is: 'For when it came to the regulations Moll was inflexible and their voice was stronger than the voice of love, in her heart, whenever they made themselves heard there simultaneously' (245). The mysterious agency or secret service headed by Youdi in *Molloy* becomes the nameless, faceless operations of the institutional asylum in *Malone Dies*, both the one where Malone currently is and the one in which Macmann ends up, if indeed they are distinct. Authority and hierarchy operate here for unknown and inscrutable reasons. Malone talks of the 'powers that be' and has no idea why they stop feeding him near the end. For all the supposed apoliticism of Beckett's worldview, in both these novels we have a deep exploration of power relationships, hierarchies and institutional domination. If the imposition of edicts from above in both novels is often comically unfathomable, it is nonetheless suffused with a menace and threat surely traceable to the bureaucratic tyrannies which Beckett witnessed at first hand.

The images of conventional day-to-day life that we are given in both *Molloy* and *Malone Dies* often depict the inhumane drudgery of everyday life. To pick one instance, Macmann witnesses the throngs of workers leaving their workplaces at the end of the day, and the scene is rendered in a third-person prose of poignant desolation, in which alienation is spliced with inarticulate familiarity:

> The doors open and spew them out, each door its contingent. For an
> instant they cluster in a daze, huddled on the sidewalk or in the gutter,
> then set off singly on their appointed ways. And even those who know
> themselves condemned, at the outset, to the same direction, for the
> choice of direction at the outset is not great, take leave of one another
> and part, but politely, with some polite excuse, or without a word, for
> they all know one another's little ways.   (211)

The workaday world of factories, businesses, farms, asylums or the police
force in the trilogy is invariably depicted as officious, inhumane, banal,
insensitive, brutish and comically self-important. So the utter failure of
Molloy or Malone to integrate themselves into this world is a sort of a virtue.
When he gets a manual job which might allow him to 'fit in', Malone
invariably messes it up spectacularly, sweeping the streets in a gloriously
incompetent manner:

> And even he himself was compelled to admit that the place swept by
> him looked dirtier at his departure than on his arrival, as if a demon
> had driven him to collect, with the broom, shovel and barrow placed
> gratis at his disposal by the corporation, all the dirt and filth which
> chance had withdrawn from the sight of the tax-payer and add them
> thus recovered to those already visible and which he was employed to
> remove.   (224)

Malone, like Molloy during his encounter with the police, tries his best to
please. But both men, in their heroic incompetence, are an affront to the
world of propriety and respectability (the 'sight of the tax-payer'). Yet
because the social world is so dehumanised, mechanical, smug and hierarchical, the misfits that so grievously fail to fit in are an implicit, and comic,
rebuke to it.

The Unnamable

Molloy and Malone have unreliable memories. Molloy knows that he is in his
mother's room, Malone knows that he is in an institution of some kind,
though neither is too sure how he got there. Both scribble their tales and
testimonies in a state of advanced perplexity. However, *The Unnamable*
explores the opacity and confusion of its predecessors at a level of unprecedented intensity. First of all, the spirit of method which so motivates Malone
in his sequenced attempts to tell his stories and perform his inventory is
avowedly spurned here: 'The thing to avoid, I don't know why, is the spirit of
system' (268). He has to talk 'in obedience to the unintelligible terms of an

incomprehensible damnation' (282), an indication that the concern with a guilt of unclear origin, together with the conflation of secular with quasi-religious imperatives, will be revisited here. The voices that Molloy hears in his head become the delegates and tormenters who prompt the Unnamable into speech, though 'they' may actually be another aspect of the speaker's fragmented selfhood.

The note of distress is sounded from the beginning, in a series of breathless questions: 'Where now? Who now? When now? Unquestioning. I, say I. Unbelieving. Questions, hypotheses, call them that' (267). The speaker talks incessantly about his predicament, but is always thwarted in his attempts to articulate it. Or, no sooner has he made an assertion about where he is or what surrounds him than he pulls it down and dismisses it as 'lies'. Moreover, each time he summons a character or a story his own identity quickly blurs into that of his creation, so that Mahood is at first a 'delegate' but then a part of himself. When he tells a story of Mahood's successor, stuck in a jar below a restaurant menu, he is both a character in a story and another description of the narrator's condition, told in the present-tense first person. Even the Unnamable himself, though he claims here, as so often elsewhere, to be reporting what 'they' are telling him, has to admit of this jar that 'its presence at such a place, about the reality of which I do not propose to quibble either, does not strike me as very credible' (316).

All these creations and narratives are ephemeral and unlikely. They evaporate and leave the Unnamable in his own desperate solitude. After the story of Mahood's ill-fated return home (which also slides into a first-person account, but is initially past tense), the Unnamable asserts testily, 'But enough of this nonsense. I was never anywhere but here, no one ever got me out of here' (297). That the veracity of the stories seems so unlikely, and that they are so readily dismissed by the teller, also and simultaneously underlines that the Unnamable is just another fictive creation himself, a product of textuality, rather than the bona fide instigator of the stories he purports to tell. Without the words on the pages, without the blackened marks, there would be no Molloy, Malone or the Unnamable. The dissolutions of selfhood that we witness in this last novel underline that these characters are no more substantial or real than their own dwindled creations. Convention dictates that we impose a hierarchy on our reading – if a character in a novel invents a story, then we often consider that story in some way less 'real' than the one in which it is nested. *The Unnamable* reveals that all is generated by the spillage of words on the page, including himself.

In his moments of clarity, he concludes ruefully that all is lies, before redirecting himself into some other cul-de-sac of abortive self-examination. What we are left with is a far more agonised, confused and desperate voice than in the first two novels of the trilogy, and a text which is much more difficult to read. However bizarre and unlikely the stories that Molloy and Malone create, the readers of the first two novels can follow their interior logic, and hence have the orientation of a coherent narrative. In *The Unnamable*, however, the thread of narrative direction is much harder to find. Furthermore the prose is far less assured, precise and serene. Its register and mood shift precipitately from sorrow to bewilderment to anger to frustration. The narrative is full of self-contradiction, shifting perspective, ambivalence and murkiness. The text does not simply give us a vision of a pared-down and degraded self, stricken and subjected to a morass of words and voices, it also enacts that condition in its own rugged textures.

Through the uncertainty, however, we find recurring and perplexing questions about the interaction between language and selfhood. Such questions are posed not from the perspective of an objective philosophical observer, but from a voice radically caught up in and subject to the contingent conditions of self-articulation and self-awareness. This novel probes the fundamentals of consciousness and self-consciousness, by shedding the naturalised sensations and perceptions which give self-consciousness, the feeling of 'I am', the impression of coherence and continuity. *The Unnamable* dismantles the famous Cartesian first principle ('I think therefore I am') by exposing the fissure between the thinking 'I' and the being 'I'. As argued above, there is no unitary 'I' that can be articulated. Once it names or identifies itself as a self, the subject is instantly fragmented into perceiver and perceived. As the Unnamable puts it early on in his verbal meanderings: 'I seem to speak, it is not I, about me, it is not about me' (267). Or near the end of the novel, 'it's the fault of the pronouns, there is no name, for me, no pronoun for me, all the trouble comes from that, that, it's a kind of pronoun too, it isn't that either, I'm not that either' (372). The multiple selves discerned by the speaking 'I' throughout the novel, the confusion between creator and creation, between first and third person, of present and past, is partly ascribable to this difficulty of speaking or articulating the self.

The problems of self-articulation also contribute to the hostility towards language and naming throughout the novel. Whilst on the one hand Beckett is a scrupulous artist and wordsmith, on the other language is presented as a 'long sin against the silence that enfolds us' (345). A puritanical dissatisfaction with artifice of any sort is an abiding feature of his mature work. In the other two novels of the trilogy there are intimations of disgust at the act of writing and story-telling. Molloy wants to 'obliterate texts', to 'fill in the holes of words till all is blank and flat and the whole ghastly business looks like what it is, senseless, speechless, issueless misery' (14). Malone, too, is frustrated by the 'tedium' of his story-telling, wants to stop telling himself 'lies' and near the end of his narrative refers to all his characters as 'pretext for not coming to the point' (254). As the immersive process of the trilogy gets deeper, the dissatisfaction with the accretions and distortions of language gets ever greater. After the war, Beckett was striving for an art based, as Krapp at thirty-nine puts it, in the 'darkness he had always strived to keep under'. But trying to say the 'unsaid' is an enterprise bound to end in failure because it inevitably changes what it is striving to express. One cannot illuminate the darkness and have it stay dark. As we have repeatedly seen in Beckett's work, language fixates and pins down its object, forsaking the fluidity and ineffability of being. This is why Beckett's work, plays and prose, tends to grow ever shorter and more minimal as his career progress. He is trying to get by with the fewest possible referents, paring back language, character and situation, since reference or representation cannot but mangle its object. The less there is to say, the better it is said.

So at crucial moments the Unnamable tries to strip away narrative, imagination, invention, leaving himself alone in the dark. 'Ah yes, all lies. God and man, nature and the light of day, the heart's outpourings and the means of understanding, all invented, basely, by me alone, with the help of no one, since there is no one, to put off the hour when I must speak of me. There will be no more about them' (278–9). This is an art in revolt against artifice, not just peeling and shedding the accoutrements of creativity and imagination, but also adopting a radical scepticism about the very foundations of perception and being in the world. It is a writing that seems to pass over, on occasion, the brink of solipsism.

So what can he say about his condition? He knows his eyes are open, because of the tears that flow from them unceasingly; he knows that he is seated, because of the pressure on his 'rump'. These descriptions of himself give way to definition, to the reintroduction of feature. He declares that his tears flow down his beard, but immediately rushes to correct himself: 'no, no beard, no hair either, it is a great smooth ball I carry on my shoulders, featureless, but for the eyes, of which only the sockets remain' (279). He strips away bodily features, the things that stick out, in his effort to shed and exfoliate the layers of illusory consolation and distraction. Renouncing all the illusions that have sustained him, there is a frantic search here for authenticity, to reach a centre or a spout of creativity, not simply to be the object of it:

Mean words, and needless, from the mean old spirit, I invented love, music, the smell of flowering currant, to escape from me. Organs, without, it's easy to imagine, a god, it's unavoidable, you imagine them, it's easy, the worst is dulled, you doze away, an instant. Yes, God, fomenter of calm, I never believed, not a second. (280)

In his efforts to strip away fictions, to access a self anterior to his narrative creation, he explicitly renounces the incarnations of the previous novels, paradoxically affirming, for the reader, a continuity between these characters and himself in the very process of denying it: 'All these Murphys, Molloys and Malones do not fool me. They have made me waste my time, suffer for nothing, speak of them when, in order to stop speaking, I should have spoken of me and of me alone' (278). Unfortunately, he comes to see at other moments that he is inextricable from these creations, that he himself is, as it were, dependent on the textual flux which he would renounce. The efforts to find an authenticity behind the narrative is thwarted as stories and personae – first (briefly) Basil, then Mahood, then Worm – obtrude into his disjointed verbiage. All the characters, and the Unnamable himself, blur into one another in his ragged, inconclusive narrative. Basil is the most hated of 'them', the voices or presences, at once tormentors, delegates and instructors, who teach the Unnamable about his mother and God, among other things, and tell him that it was in 'Bally', the Irish-sounding home town of Molloy, where 'the inestimable gift of life had been rammed down my gullet' (273). But the Unnamable decides to rename Basil, who is 'becoming important' (283) as Mahood, whose name both incorporates the idea of protective maternity and origins ('Ma'), while also gesturing towards the idea of the universal and elemental ('Manhood'). But Mahood continually merges with the Unnamable: 'It is his voice which has often, always, mingled with mine, and sometimes drowned it completely', reinforcing the broader motif of a disseminated subject, incapable of self-articulation. The characters or personae which the speaker conjures here are both part of himself and at the same time obstacles to his self-expression, 'his voice continued to testify for me, as though woven into mine, preventing me from saying who I was, what I was, so as to have done with saying, done with listening' (283).

The story about the one-legged Mahood, spiralling on his crutches around the world, quickly turns into a story about himself, told in the first person. After following expansive circles, he is finally converging on his family home. Though he is within earshot of his family's shouts of encouragement he still takes years to finish the last laps to his final destination, during which time he hears everyone in the house die excruciatingly of sausage poisoning. This story evokes some of the concerns of *Molloy*, which was also about movement and the search for origin. However, as the crippled narrator hobbles through the decayed sludge of his parents, wife and heirs, it would be difficult to imagine a more mordant, deflated and disgusted rendering of the archetypal quest for home.

He earlier promised that his next 'vice-exister' will be a 'billy in the bowl', and sure enough the next story is about a legless and armless creature stuck in a jar outside a restaurant. The menu is affixed to the jar by the proprietress of the restaurant, who also decorates it with Chinese lanterns to attract customers. Just as the movement of *Molloy* is replaced by the stillness of *Malone Dies*, *The Unnamable's* two major stories follow the sequence of the two previous novels of the trilogy in regressing from a journey to stasis. The regression is also a descent, and a shedding of physical characteristics. The creature in the jar resembles the initial faltering self-description of the speaker in the novel, his head a large featureless ball. As this is 'another of Mahood's stories . . . to be understood in the way I was given to understand it, namely as being about me' (299), it is told in the first person from the beginning. However this time it is in the present tense, whereas the spiralling journey to home and family was told in the past, reinforcing the idea that the narrative is approaching an origin or a source of some sort.

Finally this story too begins to fade, and Worm, the 'first of his kind', struggles to get born. As the accretions of physicality are shed, the creature – first and third person – gets less and less human. Still, however, the creation is at once attached to the speaker, but still preventing the 'I' from articulating itself authentically: 'I'm Worm, no, if I were Worm I wouldn't know it, I wouldn't say it, I wouldn't say anything I'd be Worm' (319). The problem, again, is one of self-articulation: 'But enough of this accursed first person, it is really too red a herring' (315). He seeks a self-integration which allows him to state the 'I' and to unify with it, a stating which will also be an entry into silence. The compulsion to speak becomes more insistent in the final sections of *The Unnamable*, words uttering forth in ever longer and more delirious sentences. The yearning to be at once defined and silent remains unavailing. The final five pages form one sustained sentence, broken into short breathless clauses, that quickens, after all the previous meandering, into a pleasingly intensified, rhythmic cadence:

> I say what I hear, I hear what I say, I don't know, one or the other, or both, that makes three possibilities, pick your fancy, all these stories about travellers, these stories about paralytics, all are mine, I must be extremely old, or it's memory playing tricks, if only I knew if I lived, if

> I live, if I'll live, that would simplify everything, impossible to find out,
> that's where you're buggered, I haven't stirred, that's all I know, no,
> I know something else, it's not I, I always forget that . . .   (380)

In this flow of clauses, which rarely exceed five words, the first person predominates, though the instability of 'I' seeps, as ever, into a confusion of pronouns, with the third person (singular and plural) often obtruding and the second person used typically, for self-reproach or imperative. There is a yearning for silence that seems, at times, both anguished and evocatively wistful. Earlier, the Unnamable referred to a duty to speak as a 'pensum' or punishment, but now the agglomeration of clauses, and the intensification of utterance, overwhelm even the mangled and impenetrable ethical system that allowed the notions of duty, obligation or sin and punishment to recur. The voice has become so mechanised that such human concerns are lost in the deterministic flow. The mood has shifted from *compulsion* to *propulsion*. This is not to say that volition has entirely departed the voice or voices that we hear in this final insistent murmur. However, the mechanical quality here, the sense of a severely suspended and contingent selfhood, resistant to totality or unity, is very much at odds with conventional notions of the individual self or its capacity to exert moral agency.

   The last line of *The Unnamable* is one of the most famous lines in Beckett's canon. Quoted out of context, it can sometimes be misread as a statement of Kiplingesque fortitude, with its determination to 'go on'. It is much more radical, much less complacently reassuring than this implies, coming as it does at the end of a text which queries the integrity of the self, the unity of experience and the validity of any authority: 'it will be I, it will be the silence, where I am, I don't know, I'll never know, in the silence you don't know, you must go on, I can't go on, I'll go on' (382).

How It Is

How It Is was Beckett's first 'novel' (or novel-length prose work) for ten years. The palpable sense of effort and struggle that went into its composition is reproduced in the effort it demands from the reader. Treating a man pulling himself laboriously through the mud, this is a text about strain and effort on many levels. *The Unnamable* could hardly be described as an easy or accessible novel, but even in the final frantic pages, when sentences are abandoned for a pulsing stream of utterance, the commas are still there to divide the clauses and guide us towards the sense and meaning. *How It Is* has no punctuation, no commas, no full stops and is narrated in short, spasmodic paragraphs of irregular length. The paragraphs, or rather chunks of prose, signal a caesura but they don't always mark the closing of sense. Sometimes a sentence continues into the next paragraph, as if it is traversing stanzas. The prose within the paragraphs is delivered in short breathless phrases, with much repetition. In order to determine meaning, the reader must infer where the breakages or stoppages in the prose should come. In this sense the reader of *How It Is* is implicated in the creative process, inferring or mentally adding the missing pauses and restoring the implicit punctuation. Therefore, to read the novel is, in a sense, to finish writing it – an appropriate phenomenon for a text that so obdurately confuses creator and creation, imagination and reality, writing and the body. The narrative, in this way, visits its themes in its method.

However, despite this ambiguity and difficulty in the prose the text also has the extreme meticulousness and purity that we have come to associate with Beckett's later work. It is spare and wintry, but there are shafts of extraordinary vividness of description, and a scrupulous attention to rhythm and prosody. The repetition of phrases – 'murmur in the mud', 'I say it as I hear it', 'vast stretch of time' and so on – increase the sense of a rhythmic, strophic effect. Thematically, there are clear continuities with Beckett's earlier work: the fissured self, the alienation from the different selves that make up the subject's past, the inadequacy of words to express silence, the master–slave feature of human relationships, the purgatorial, non-realist setting, the voices in the head: all are familiar Beckettian concerns, despite the new direction that language and structure has taken here. Moreover, this is not a literature weighed down with obscure allusions to other writers or works (the few there are tend to proliferate in Part 1). The difficulties the text presents lie in the slippery word patterns and the ambiguity of sense, not in arcane or erudite reference. The attentive reader can decode the complexity of the text without recourse to annotation.

That said, even after grappling with the unpunctuated prose, the reader might well be perplexed by the situation described in the text. From now on the setting of Beckett's prose texts becomes ever more detached from even the residual recognisability of the trilogy. A speaker face down in the mud and darkness drags himself painfully forward pulling behind him a sack containing tins of sardines and a tin-opener, tied at the mouth with a rope, which is in turn tied to his neck. He describes voices, first coming from the outside, then from the inside 'when the panting stops'. In Part 2 he stumbles on Pim, also prostrate in the mud, and their time together is marked both by the eroticism of their encounter and the sadism that the speaker shows towards his fellow, especially as he tries to communicate with him. In Part 3, when Pim moves away at last, the speaker slowly realises that he is awaiting his own tormenter, Bom, who will treat him as he has treated Pim. At first, the speaker comes to the conclusion that there are millions of such couples wriggling in the mud, enacting this sequence of tormenter and tormented. However, at the end of the text (like at the end of *The Unnamable*) he declares that all is invention and that the voices he hears and the characters he has evoked are simply the result of his own feverish imaginings. He is utterly alone.

The speaker of *How It Is* begins his narrative by highlighting the voices around him:

> how it was I quote before Pim with Pim after Pim how it is three parts I say is as I hear it
>> voice once without quaqua on all sides then in me when the panting stops tell me again finish telling me invocation   (7)

If we are to believe him, the story of *How It Is* is told not by the speaker but by the voices without and within. The phrases 'I say it as I hear it' and 'I say them as I hear them' are leitmotifs in the narrative, reinforcing the importance of extrinsic (or intrinsic) voices as a narrative source. In one sense 'I say it as I hear it' (a phrase first used in 'Text V' from *Texts for Nothing*) is a testament of fidelity: 'I am saying just what I hear and not bearing false witness.' In another, it is a disavowal or a disowning of what he hears: 'Do not blame me for what I am saying. I am only the messenger.'

It is common in Beckett's post-war work for the narrative to set out its own structure, or planned structure, in advance – a reassuring glimpse of order in a chaotic world. Malone, for instance, has a carefully worked-though sequence for his final flourishes. *How It Is* also starts out with a plan. The speaker tells us that this story, a retrospective account of 'how it was' told in the present tense, will be divided into a three-part narrative sequence. However, while Malone botches up his plan and expires before he can properly perform his inventory, *How It Is*, for all its strain and struggle, manages to achieve its anticipated structure. It does follow a tripartite before-Pim, with-Pim, after-Pim narrative sequence, signalled by the shift in parts. It is an unusual success in the very common search among Beckett's characters for a system.

What, then, of the setting, the world of mud and darkness in which the speaker struggles, only occasionally being granted images of life above in the light? From the Italian poet Giacomo Leopardi (1798–1837), Beckett had culled the epigraph to *Proust*: '*E fango è il mondo*' ('The world is mud'). Now he is deploying this description as a literal condition. He speaks of another life, significantly the life 'above in the light said to have been mine', whereas now he is in 'the mud the dark the silence the solitude'. The opening of Part 1 is interspersed with flashes and images from this 'life in the light' though there is 'no going back up there' (8). He murmurs these memories into the mud in which he is now immersed, though he insists that they are images that are given to him rather than memories over which he has any control. This submerged, dark place, without any possibility of dying of hunger or thirst during this 'vast stretch of time', evokes a purgatory or hell of some sort.

However, if the scene here evokes an after-life, it could also be associated with an ancient or pre-evolved world: 'warmth of primeval mud impenetrable dark' (12). The characters here, though with human features, also resemble pre-mammalian reptiles wriggling in the mud: the references to the natural order and the vast stretches of time evokes that massive period of world history before developed life. There is a mention of the German evolutionary theorist Ernst Haeckel (1834–1919), famed for his theory that 'ontogeny recapitulates phylogeny', that the development of the foetus goes through the various evolutionary stages of the species (47). Moreover, the original French title, *Comment c'est*, puns on *commencer* (to start). The text evokes primeval *and* purgatorial worlds, before and after life. As so often in Beckett, beginnings and endings, birth and death, are conflated. The associations of setting are multiple and indefinite. One should not close off another.

Images from the speaker's life (if they are from his life) flash in front of him: cutting up butterflies' wings as a child (10), sitting in a room with a woman who watches him as she embroiders at the table, initially content that he is 'working', then suddenly taking fright at his seeming immobility (11). These evocations are not dreams, the narrator assures us, nor are they memories, but rather images of 'the kind I sometimes see in the mud' (11). Significantly, he is keen to disown the images he sees, as much as the voices he hears. A little later however, he has another image. It is of his mother's face:

> I see it from below it's like nothing I ever saw
>
> we are on a veranda smothered in verbena the scented sun dapples the red tiles yes I assure you
>
> the huge head hatted with birds and flowers is bowed down over my curls the eyes burn with severe love I offer her mine pale upcast to the sky whence cometh our help and which I know perhaps even then with time shall pass away
>
> in a word bolt upright on a cushion on my knees whelmed in a nightshirt I pray according to her instructions

> that's not all she closes her eyes and drones a snatch of the so-called
> Apostles' Creed I steal a look at her lips
>
> she stops her eyes burn down on me again I cast up mine in haste and
> repeat awry
>
> the air thrills with the hum of insects
> that's all it goes out like a lamp blown out   (16–17)

The scene, as many critics point out, corresponds with of one of the youngest photographs of Beckett, kneeling at his mother's feet on a cushion in the veranda of his childhood home (though in the photograph, his head is bowed in a posed prayer, not looking into his mother's eyes).[6] Beckett could hardly have such a vivid memory at so young an age, so he probably borrowed the image from the photograph. Like the later scenes of Pim's 'education' in Part 2, this image combines intimacy and domination, love and severity. The final sustained image of Part 1 is of the speaker aged sixteen at the racecourse on a spring day, hand in hand with a girlfriend, who has a dog on a leash. The couple initially have their back to the narrator, which in part explains the latter's fascination with his own youthful posterior, 'the arse I have', he repeatedly muses. However, they turn around, allowing the narrator to comment on his face and legs. Like all the images of life above in the light, this scene suddenly appears and is suddenly cut, like an abruptly edited film. Here is a pastoral love scene, a rural setting with sheep spotting the surrounding hills, but it is also profoundly parodic. The movements are full of a mechanical, clockwork quality that contradicts the ostensible romantic and bucolic atmosphere. The speaker is recording them from a set position, like a fixed camera, as they 'about turn introrse at ninety degrees' (33). The couple eat their sandwiches at alternate bites, one swallowing as the other bites. It is a scene which resurfaces, in fragments, in Parts 1 and 3. However clockwork and celluloid the scene, it has a brightness and vividness that seems pre-lapsarian compared with the life in the mud.

The final movements in the mud in Part 1, before the encounter with Pim and the start of Part 2, are also described in a mechanical, spatially regulated idiom. The carefully measured objects of description contrast with the unpunctuated and confusing method of description as the clarity and light of the speaker's visions contrast with the mud and struggle in which he lives:

> semi-side right left leg left arm push pull flat on the face mute
> imprecations scrabble in the mud every half-yard eight times per
> chevron or three yards of headway clear a little less the hand dips
> clawing for the take instead of the familiar slime an arse two cries one
> mute end of part one before Pim that's how it was before Pim   (54)

But after this encounter with Pim, at the start of Part 2, he immediately resolves to drop his interest in measurement and numbering: 'no more figures there's another little difference compared to what precedes not the slightest figure henceforth all measures vague' (57). It seems that human encounter removes the need for abstract measurement. As soon as his hand falls on Pim's arse his capacity for (or interest in) measuring time and space decreases: 'smartly as from a block of ice or white-hot my hand recoils hangs a moment it's vague in mid air then slowly sinks again and settles firm' (57). Measurement has become 'vague' – in Part 3 it will return forcefully, as for pages and pages he tries desperately to work out the combinations and configurations of the millions of couplings of tormenter and victims that he imagines in this underworld. The mathematical conundrums he comes up with at this late stage, and the doggedness with which he tries to solve them, evoke the similar yearning for symmetry of Watt or Molloy. The stable act of counting forms a refuge or a retreat from the unstable, unreliable business of recounting. This urge for numerical certainty is a compensation for the lack of certainty of language – 'something wrong there' is the refrain for the speaker's reflections on what he has just said.

On a basic level this is a narrative about an utterly solitary and debilitated man meeting a fellow sufferer. Their initial meeting, with the speaker groping around Pim's naked body, is charged with sexual discovery. This is amongst Beckett's most homo-erotic texts: 'we're a pair my right arm presses him against me love fear of being abandoned a little of each no knowing not said' (73). There is intimacy, sexual exploration, fascination, but as this is a Beckett text, we know not to expect too many pat affirmations of fellowship or community. Discovery and identification mutate into and co-exist with casual torment and subjection of the other. 'DO YOU LOVE ME CUNT' (99) are the last few words that are gouged into Pim's back, encapsulating the ambivalence. Typically in Beckett, human relations are mordantly undercut with humorous if shocking cruelty, which is not to say that fellow-feeling is abolished altogether.

The speaker extracts both song and cries of pain from his hapless fellow by ingenious systems of physical torture: nails in the armpit causes song, the tin-opener driven into arse-cheek elicits cries and then speech, the pestle in the kidneys prompts more volume; when he makes the wrong sound, or when he is required to stop, the thump on the skull is deployed. It is a brutal form of education. Verbal communication is followed by written – the narrator starts to write on Pim's back with his nails, 'from left to right and top to bottom as in our civilization I carve my Roman capitals' (77).

In its move from primitive guttural sound to speech to writing, Pim's training in a sense recapitulates the progression of human civilisation. This might be another echo of the word *commencer*. We find not just the beginnings of the 'natural order', or the emergence of humankind from the slime, but also the evolution of the cultural order. This beginning is accompanied, indeed transmitted, by the barbaric methods of Pim's indoctrination. It seems that the origins of culture, as well as those of nature, are red in tooth and claw. The implication may be that civilisation, writing and literature grow out of historical brutality. Most civilisations, and hence the written cultures they generate, emerge through war, conquest and slavery and subjection, after all. 'There is no document of civilization', as Walter Benjamin famously puts it, 'which is not at the same time a document of barbarism.'[7]

Writing on the body, as the body of Pim is written on by the speaker in Part 2, is an image almost custom-made for the post-structuralist critic. It is a metaphor for the inseparability of subjectivity from text. There is no real Pim, or Bom or Bem – they are illusions generated by language. The same is true for all fictional characters. Beckett has always spurned the naturalistic conventions of traditional fiction, but perhaps nowhere else has he provided so vivid an image of the literal textualisation of one of his characters. His body is identified explicitly as the receptacle for the language of the narrator. As Pim speaks, the speaker writes – both forms of language come after all only through the words that we are reading on the page. The identification between the two is increased, reinforcing that familiar device in Beckett's prose whereby one character's quest for or encounter with another often yields to a blurring between the two, so that one self becomes indistinguishable from the other. The speaker starts to feel that, in the order of things, he too will one day lie like Pim and a certain Bom will come along, with sack and tin opener, and treat him in the manner he has treated Pim. 'I too Pim my name Pim,' the speaker at one stage declares. But at another moment he claims that it is he who is Bom. All the characters are the products of the same textual flow, the same slippery effulgence of the words on these pages. Hence the closeness of their names and of their identities:

> we're talking of me not Pim Pim is finished he has finished me now
> part three not Pim my voice not his saying this these words can't go on
> and Pim that Pim never was and Bom whose coming I await to finish be
> finished have finished me too that Bom will never be no Pim no Bom
> and this voice quaqua of us all never was only one voice my voice never any
> other   (95)

In Part 3 the speaker strives for some understanding of the genesis of his condition. There was a time before Part 1, when the speaker played Pim's part and Bem performed the role of tormenter. The speaker thinks through the sequences of tormenter and victim: he left Bem to reach Pim, and now awaits Bom since Pim has left and Pim crawls towards another victim, for whom he will act as tormenter. The mania for symmetry, arithmetic and order, which the speaker abandoned on encountering Pim, forcefully returns here, especially as he tries to work out the number of victims and tormenters that exist in this world. It is as if he seeks the cool certainties of measurement as a balm for his renewed solitude. But the symmetry does not quite fit, as ever there is 'something wrong here'. If the victim leaves his sack when he finally crawls away from his tormenter, then how come he is dragging a sack as he crawls to his own victim?

At the end the niggling doubts ('something wrong here') and the faltering faith in the procedures of his own narrative burst out in complete renunciation. The whole tale is false:

> all these calculations yes explanations yes the whole story from beginning to end yes completely false yes
>
> that wasn't how it was no not at all no how then no answer how was it then no answer HOW WAS IT screams good
>
> there was something yes but nothing of all that no all balls from start to finish yes this voice quaqua yes all balls yes only one voice here yes mine yes when the panting stops yes   (158)

All the voices, all the characters – Pim, Bom, Krik, Kram – all the images from the world above, all is dismissed at the end of the text as 'balls'.

The title of the novel, then, has to be considered as ironic. The speaker is left with the stricken recognition of his own sheer aloneness. In the play *Not I* the female protagonist wants to avoid using the word 'I' and is appalled when the first person intrudes. The dissolution of masks, voices and invented selves leads, as so often, to a similar awareness of the loneliness, isolation and alienation of the unconsoled self. But if the speaker declares that everything he says is 'balls', all his descriptions mere inventions, then how are we to tell that this statement too is not invention? How are we to know that the passage quoted above is not just as unreliable as all the other textual inventions? When he contradicts his earlier claim that everything he says comes from voices outside him how are we to know that he is not simply quoting the outer voice? Like the final episode of Joyce's *Ulysses* (to which there is at least one allusion), the third part of *How It Is* unravels the textual weave, leaving us, as so often in Beckett's prose, with a pained, fragmented voice flickering on in radical indeterminacy.

Chapter 5

Beckett criticism

The shape of Beckett's career tends towards attenuation, his works getting ever sparer and more pointed as he got older. The less there is to say, it seems, the better it is said. By contrast, the criticism and commentary his work has produced have ballooned into hundreds of monographs and thousands of articles, far too many for a brief survey such as this. There are two specialist journals wholly devoted to Beckett scholarship, *Journal of Beckett Studies* and *Samuel Beckett Today / Aujourd'hui,* and a steady stream of conferences and symposia. One could point at a number of reasons for this academic interest. Initially his work was perceived as profoundly concerned with fundamental questions about the nature of human existence. Though this approach (which we might describe as 'humanist', assuming as it does that the experience of human existence is a constant across different cultures and historical periods) has diminished in the anti-essentialist bias of much modern literary theory, the aura around Beckett's work of the elemental, the bravely confrontational and the enduringly profound has certainly not dissipated. Secondly, the notorious difficulty of Beckett's work, be it the erudition of the early fiction or the alienating and purgatorial settings of the later prose and drama, is also a lure for critics and scholars, as there is clearly a need for their presence. With all the uncertainty and allusiveness, scholars have much to explain and annotate. This is surely one of the reasons why so many of the major modernist (and 'difficult') authors have received so much academic attention. Add to the profundity and the difficulty of Beckett's world the formal inventiveness, the questioning of the basic structures of drama and fiction, and the incentive for critical and scholarly response becomes irresistible. Beckett's refusal to comment on or offer explication of his work has fuelled the interest and the mystique surrounding him, which has in turn prompted more critical attention. Perhaps more than any other modern author he is revered as somewhere between a saint and a seer, a figure of insight and uncompromising artistic integrity. The attitude of veneration may well have hobbled the judicious scepticism that healthy literary criticism sometimes needs. His few gnomic critical utterances have been endlessly

116

quoted and requoted, invested with an authority over his work that the critical comments of a less iconic literary figure would not be given. Moreover, it may have abetted the tendency to regard him as having transcended the historical and social conditions from which he writes, to see his work as about the human condition, rather than an expression of a historically specific crisis of value.

Another reason why Beckett has prompted so much critical fascination is because his work can be persuaded to fit into any number of models or systems. Beckett's stripped stages and rootless contexts have resulted in his enlistment into many critical or theoretical movements over the last fifty years. It was almost as if the deracinated settings turned Beckett's work into a mirror in which a multitude of critical methods and schools could find their own reflections. Existentialists found a concern with human isolation and the absurdity of the universe, while narrative theorists pointed at the metatextual interest in the construction and unravelling of stories. Post-structuralists celebrated in Beckett the self-reflexive consciousness of textuality and a concern with shape, repetition, the forming and deforming aspects of language, while hermeneuticists pored over the abiding concern with interpretation and how meaning is generated from language and the world. Religious critics focused on the concern with spirituality and the deployment of religious and even mystical language and psychoanalytic critics found a first-person narrator gabbling out its memories like a patient to a therapist. All this is in no way to imply that the capacity to generate a variety of critical responses is to be lamented. It is rather the sign of important and enduring work.

Beckett criticism has mainly accrued in three languages: English, French and German. The main focus of this short survey will be the English-language criticism, which, in terms of full-length studies, began in the 1960s. Early Beckett criticism, as already indicated, tended to see Beckett in broadly existentialist terms, as a playwright who had something fundamental to say about the 'human condition'. It was often philosophical in its orientation, because of the existentialist comparison, because of the allegorical readings that accrued around the early plays, and because of the philosophical allusions to Descartes and others evident in the early prose. This philosophical approach was complemented by a formalist or new critical attention to the structures and language of the work. Often humanist ideas about meaning and formalist methods of close-reading were deployed in the same critical work.

The critic who, over a long career, has given most sustained attention to Beckett, from her *Samuel Beckett: The Comic Gamut* (1962), through *Back to*

Beckett (1973) and *Just Play: Samuel Beckett's Theatre* and on to, most recently, *A Beckett Canon* (2001), is Ruby Cohn. Indeed, if one were to pick a starting point for academic Beckett studies in English, the special issue of *Perspective* (vol. 11, no. 3, 1959), edited by Cohn and devoted to Beckett's work, would be an obvious one. Her work ranks alongside Hugh Kenner's as inaugurating Beckett studies. Her first book usefully ensured that the complexities of Beckettian comedy (studied with reference to French theorist of comedy Henri Bergson) were not lost in the emphasis on meaninglessness and absurdity elsewhere in Beckett studies. Kenner's *Samuel Beckett: A Critical Study* (1961) was the first book-length study of Beckett whose emphasis on Descartes and philosophical aspects of his work would prove highly influential. Kenner argued that the mind–body split was at the heart of Beckett's work. 'The Cartesian Centaur', an oft-reprinted chapter from this book, argues that the man on a bicycle, which is so prevalent in Beckett's work, is a metaphor for this dualism, the bicycle an extension of the wholly mechanical qualities of the body. As Beckett's work progresses the harmony between mind and body, rider and bicycle, breaks down. By the time of *The Unnamable*, 'The bicycle is long gone, the Centaur dismembered; of the exhilaration of the cyclist's progress in the days when he was the lord of the things that move, nothing remains but the ineradicable habit of persisting like a machine.'[1]

   Martin Esslin published *The Theatre of the Absurd* in 1961, the same year as Kenner's first book, but in 1965 also published *Samuel Beckett: A Collection of Critical Essays*. Esslin's introduction to this collection has been described as 'undoubtedly the most influential fifteen pages in the history of Beckett criticism'.[2] To its credit, this 'Introduction' stresses Beckett's interest in shape and form and resists the tendency to translate Beckett's art into abstract philosophical ideas: 'an artist like Beckett does not concern himself with abstract and general verities'.[3] In the process, Kierkegaard and Kafka are fruitfully brought to bear on a reading of Beckett's work as a whole. The essay also embodies the inclination in these early days to find something paradoxically uplifting in Beckett's work. Beckett is often revered for a sort of existential bravery for his courage and resilience in facing the absurdity of existence without turning his gaze. His vision may be bleak, but there is an integrity, even a heroism, in looking at the horror without yielding to false consolation. Esslin puts it thus:

> To be in communication with a mind of such merciless integrity, of such uncompromising determination to face the stark reality of the human situation and to confront the worst without ever being in

danger of yielding to any of the superficial consolations that have clouded man's self awareness in the past [. . .] to partake of such courage and noble stoicism, however remotely, cannot but evoke a feeling of emotional excitement, exhilaration.[4]

Strikingly, Esslin here both invokes history by referring to the superficial consolations of the past, but eschews it in implying that Beckett has achieved some universal vision of the 'human situation' that less brave, enlightened or bleak ages have missed. But surely the discourses of confrontation and emotional excitement may themselves be culturally located, may indeed be a 'superficial consolation' of the implicitly post-theistic age from which he writes. For instance could the notion of facing down the 'worst' not belong to a post-World War ethic, though the need for endurance and bravery has now shifted onto an existential plane? In other words the values of the Blitz – resilience, bravery, fortitude against the odds – are still percolating around the culture in the fifties and sixties and allow the 'noble stoicism' in the face of the absurdity of the 'human situation' to give some succour.

For many later critics, the tendency to talk about the 'human situation' amongst the first generation of Beckett critics, or to speak of an existence that is universally shared and experienced, tends to exclude the historical mediation of human feeling and human experience. More politically accented criticism would tend to be suspicious of such trans-historical and essentialist views, denying that it is possible to speak about what it means to be human outside the constructions of specific social and historical conditions. Human experience, it would hold, is not a constant: it differs in different times and places. The experience of an Aztec Indian is wholly incomparable to that of a New York stockbroker or a stone-age hunter gatherer and it is fallacious to assume that a post-war twentieth-century writer with a pessimistic outlook speaks for them all. What is missing, then, may be a more developed incorporation of the historical situation from which Beckett writes.

One should, however, be wary of too brisk a dismissal of the critical assumptions of the first wave of Beckett critics. It is always too easy to yield to the Oedipal temptation to topple the preceding generation, especially when Beckett criticism is so crowded, and critics feel a need to stake out their own territory. Cohn, Kenner and Esslin are still indispensable guides to Beckett's work, their procedures and insights often far more subtle than the humanist or essentialist caricature allows. Indeed, it is striking how often in their work one finds a passage or an interpretation which anticipates many of the supposedly more radical, post-structuralist approaches of the eighties and nineties.

The Beckett industry expanded and consolidated as the years went by, especially after the award of the Nobel Prize to Beckett in 1969. Specialised works on the prose or drama became more common, like Eugene Webb's two books, *Samuel Beckett: A Study of his Novels* (1970) and his companion volume *The Plays of Samuel Beckett* (1972). H. Porter Abbott's *The Fiction of Samuel Beckett: Form and Effect* (1973) and James Knowlson's *Light and Darkness in the Theatre of Samuel Beckett* (1972) are also important examples. Deserving of special mention in the specialist camp, not least because of the unprecedented access to interviews and conversations with Beckett himself, is Lawrence Harvey's *Samuel Beckett: Poet and Critic* (1970). For all its unwieldy organisation, it is also an extensively annotated account of sources for the still neglected poetry, criticism and early prose.

Though Beckett criticism in the 1970s was more split along the lines of prose and drama than hitherto, there was still intense interest in the philosophical coordinates of the work as a whole. David Hesla's *The Shape of Chaos: An Interpretation of the Art of Samuel Beckett* (1971) is still a useful guide to the intellectual and philosophical background, especially in relation to the prose works. John Pilling's *Samuel Beckett* (1976) offers not just a comprehensive and informed account of the various influences on Beckett, philosophical and literary, together with sensitive readings of the works, it also provides a detailed cartography of the larger cultural contexts in which Beckett's work can be located. James Knowlson and John Pilling's *Frescoes of the Skull: The Later Prose and Drama of Samuel Beckett* (1979) sought to complement the sizeable commentary on Beckett's middle period by focusing on the later texts from *How It Is* onwards, together with earlier works which had not yet been published, namely *Dream of Fair to Middling Women* and *Eleutheria*.

The 1980s saw literary theory go mainstream in English departments and a surge of readings of Beckett's work inspired by post-structuralism and deconstruction. This decade also saw the highpoint of the debate about whether Beckett should be grouped with the modernists or the postmodernists. His characters are clearly bewildered and insatiable story-tellers, but they rarely succeed in either a competent story or any assurance that their ramblings relate to a coherent world. The question, simply put, is whether the stories should be regarded as inadequate instruments, not fulfilling the need to articulate or express a condition. In which case, though language is doomed to fail in its obligation to express, there is nonetheless an ineffable reality behind it. Or are they rather constitutive, generating the reality that they purport to articulate, one story yielding into another without any 'real' world anterior to the system of signs spilling onto the page? So often in the trilogy and *How It Is*, after all, the characters renounce what they say as fictions. To return to the discussion of *Molloy*, should we emphasise the 'nameless things' of modernism or the 'thingless names' of postmodernism? It should be emphasised, again, that this question was not new in Beckett studies. The blurring of the distinction between art and life, language and reality, is treated even in the earliest studies. The instability of meaning, the fraught relationship between names and their objects and the idea that language often invented what it pretended to describe were considered even in the earliest Beckett criticism of Ruby Cohn.

The move, then, into post-structuralist readings of Beckett was not a revolution so much as an increased emphasis on these linguistic contours, on the constitutive power of textuality. The modernist Beckett emphasises the need for formal innovation and experiment to articulate a recalcitrant and chaotic world, to confront the 'mess' with the inevitably shoddy tools that language and literary form allow. The postmodernist Beckett distrusts the idea that the name comes after the thing at all, claiming instead that language constructs its object. For the modernist, the Beckettian character says, or fails to say, something *about* the self; for the postmodernist he or she *says* the self. In other words, subjectivity, or the 'I', only comes into being through language, through the speaking self. 'I, say I', as the Unnamable puts it (267). There is no self anterior to the speaking self; language makes the self, it does not simply reflect it. Human experience is not described by narrative or story-telling, it is formed by this process. It is impossible to conceive of a non-narrative human experience – to conceive of it we must enter a textual web of exclusions, inconsistencies, omissions, value judgements and so on. Texts do not simply reproduce experiences; the postmodernist would emphasise the textual nature *of* experience itself.

Postmodernist discourse often likes to topple conceptual hierarchies, perhaps never more so than the priority of the original or the authentic over the copy or the fake. Repetition or replication clearly undermines this priority as the original gets lost and ever more displaced each time it is repeated. Steven Connor's *Samuel Beckett: Repetition, Theory and Text* (1988) analyses themes and tropes of repetition in Beckett's work to show how it refuses and subverts authentic or original human experience. Other examples of postmodernist or post-structuralist approaches to Beckett include Angela Moorjani's *Abysmal Games in the Novels of Samuel Becket* (1982), Leslie Hill's *Beckett's Fiction: In Different Words* (1990) and Carla Locatelli's *Unwording the Word: Samuel Beckett's Prose Works After the Nobel Prize* (Philadelphia: University of Pennsylvania Press, 1990).

Though there are real differences between the modernist and postmodernist positions, we should perhaps be wary of too great a reliance on imposed literary or intellectual categories like these. Beckett does not have to exclusively 'belong' to one or other, and there is evidence in his work to support both positions. Moreover talk of critical or theoretical turf wars between Beckett the modernist and Beckett the postmodernist sometimes underestimates the continuity between the approaches. Deconstructionist studies may have deployed more overtly theoretical models than hitherto, they may have ruptured the idea of the texts as being self-contained by showing how they draw on a wider network of signs and structures, but many continued the tendency to read Beckett in textual or formalist terms, however porous or unstable the text was now supposed to be. Both approaches tended towards a reluctance to theorise Beckett's context, to try to relocate his seemingly rootless sets or mystifying prose worlds into social conditions or historical critique.

Furthermore the aura surrounding Beckett evinced in previous critical perspectives is maintained in the post-structuralist era, though with a somewhat different spin. Whereas the critics of the early 1960s celebrated Beckett for his existential heroism, for his brave confrontation of the abyss, critics of the 1980s celebrated Beckett's resistance to closure, to convention, to certainty. It was precisely the lack of rootedness or essentialism in his work, its refusal of all sorts of totality, its radical questioning of many of the assumptions of Western metaphysics that win the praise of a theorised criticism suspicious of hegemonic thought structures locked into patterns of domination and subordination. There is a political dimension to this, more or less articulated. Beckett's unravelling of fixed and stable meanings loosens the hierarchical logic that enforces the binary thinking behind subject and object, ruler and ruled, man and woman, self and other.

Some critics taking a post-structuralist view have developed the political implications of Beckett's work more than others. Steven Connor, as already seen, argues that the repetition in Beckett's work has a subversive anti-hegemonic undertow. In the 1990s there was a reflux against the postmodern idea of Beckett as detached from the 'real world' even from critics who were themselves theoretically informed. H. Porter Abbot's *Beckett Writing Beckett: The Author in the Autograph* (1996) opposes those who would see Beckett's writing as simply an elaborate game by pointing at the 'intense earnestness that distinguishes him from so many of his postmodern contemporaries'.[5] Later in this engaging and thoughtful book, Abbott devotes a chapter exclusively to the discussion of 'Political Beckett' in which he considers the various ways in which this issue might be addressed.[6]

Psychoanalytic approaches, especially those of Freud, Jung and Lacan, have long found rich pickings in Beckett's works. He had, after all, undergone psychoanalysis himself in the 1930s and read deeply in the area around this time. Phil Baker's important book *Beckett and the Mythology of Psychoanalysis* (1997) was a breakthrough in this field because it merged a psychoanalytical approach with a consciousness of historical location. In other words it did not use psychoanalysis as a source of mythic truth, nor as a form of 'simplistic psychobiography', but rather as an historically formed set of intellectual phenomena: 'There is a whole retrospective landscape of loss in mid-twentieth century culture,' claims Baker, 'constituted by notions such as the paradise of the womb, pre-Oedipal plenitude, paternal prohibition, oceanic regression, narcissism, and the narratives of mourning and melancholia.'[7] His book situates Beckett within this landscape.

Feminist criticism of Beckett has, arguably, teased out the political and social implication of post-structuralist approaches to Beckett more than any other. In 1990 Linda Ben-Zvi edited a collection entitled *Women in Beckett: Performance and Critical Perspectives.* Mary Bryden's *Women in Samuel Beckett's Prose and Drama* (1994) deploys the work of French feminist and postmodern theorists, including Julia Kristeva, Gilles Deleuze and Felix Guattari. She argues that there is a progression in Beckett's work from the essentialist association of woman with the body in Beckett's early prose to a much more fluid, contingent and politically progressive notion of gender identity in the later works.

David Lloyd claims that Beckett's work 'stands as the most exhaustive dismantling we have of the logic of identity that at every level structures and maintains the post-colonial moment'.[8] Surprisingly enough, given the growth in post-colonial theory in recent years, there have been surprisingly few attempts to read Beckett in post-colonial terms after Lloyd's article. With all the uncertain subjectivity, alienation, self-conscious marginality, repetition and mimicry in Beckett's world, one might have thought he would be ripe for such treatment. Part of the reason has to do with Beckett's Irishness, and the resistance to it, which I treated in Chapter 2. Earlier full-length treatments such as Eoin O'Brien's *The Beckett Country* (1986) and John Harrington's academic study *The Irish Beckett* (1991) met a lukewarm response from some Beckett critics of formalist persuasion. Declan Kiberd's *Inventing Ireland: The Literature of the Modern Nation* (1995), a hugely influential text in recent Irish studies that draws on post-colonial models, lays claim to Beckett as 'the first truly Irish playwright, because the first utterly free of factitious elements of Irishness'.[9] Apart from these few moments, however, Irish studies have only picked up fleetingly on Beckett, while Beckett studies have only momentarily nodded at Beckett's Irishness.

However, even in books (like Baker's) not overtly addressing the issue, there was a renewed emphasis on context and history in the 1990s. Perhaps this has something to do with the lessening of Beckett's closeness to us in historical terms. It surely also has something to do with a turn towards history in the study of literature generally, with the rise of what came to be known as the 'new historicism'. But even within Beckett studies itself there were mould-breaking developments that made the context from which his works emerged impossible to ignore. Chief amongst these has been the publication in 1996 of an authorised biography of Beckett by James Knowlson, *Damned to Fame: The Life of Samuel Beckett*. Unlike its 1978 predecessor by Deirdre Bair, Knowlson's biography was written with Beckett's assistance, including multiple interviews with its subject and unprecedented access to previously unseen papers. Foremost amongst these were the German Diaries that Beckett had kept during his tours around Germany in 1936–7. Knowlson's biography has opened up Beckett studies in the last ten years, giving us the man and his work far more situated and in context than the myth of the seer-like artist, producing timeless expressions of human misery, would allow. Knowlson's emphasis on the influence of other art forms on Beckett, especially music and painting, has opened up fresh seams in the study of Beckett's aesthetic that has been tapped by two edited collections, Mary Bryden's *Samuel Beckett and Music* (1998) and Lois Oppenheim's *Samuel Beckett and the Arts: Music, Visual Arts and Non-Print Media* (1999). Daniel Albright is a modernist scholar who has long investigated the connections between literary and non-literary, particularly musical, modes. His *Beckett and Aesthetics* (2003) brings this background to bear on a detailed study of Beckett's struggle with artistic media.

1996 was a bumper year for Beckett biographies. Anthony Cronin's, *Samuel Beckett: The Last Modernist* (1996), is a substantial achievement, particularly illuminating on Beckett's Irish context. Lois Gordon's *The World of Samuel Beckett 1906–1946* (1996) emphasised the various historical crises that he lived through. John Pilling's *Beckett Before Godot: The Formative Years 1929–1946* (1998) was also contextual, providing a learned analysis of the gestation of Beckett's writing in the years preceding his great post-war creative outburst with reference to a wealth of unpublished manuscripts from around the world. The publication of Beckett's correspondence with his American director Alan Schneider in 1998 (edited by Maurice Harmon) has whetted the appetite for a collected letters, due out in the near future, a resource that can only assist our ongoing location of Beckett within his own times.

Biographical and contextual work like this relies heavily on archival resources. The variety of Beckett criticism outlined above coexists with, and has often been penetrated and informed by, archival and scholarly work devoted to Beckett. Many of Beckett's notebooks, manuscripts, drafts, correspondence, theatre ephemera and so on have been donated to or bought by various universities around the world, including the University of Reading (under the aegis of the Beckett International Foundation), the University of Texas at Austin, Trinity College Dublin, Washington University, St Louis, and Dartmouth College, New Hampshire, and these archives have proved a rich mine for scholars and researchers. Richard L. Admussen's *The Samuel Beckett Manuscripts* (1979) was a pioneering map of these archives, which have proved so useful to Beckett scholarship in the 1980s and 1990s. One of the most significant manuscript-based studies is S. E. Gontarski's *The Intent of Undoing in Samuel Beckett's Dramatic Texts* (1985), which demonstrated that Beckett tended to shed references to a recognisable or realistic world as the various drafts of a work proceeded. The rootless Beckettian scene came about as a result of a conscious winnowing-down, a deliberate dislocation from the conventional realism of surface appearances and logical relations.

Another extremely significant contribution from archives was the publication of the various 'theatrical notebooks' Beckett kept when directing his own plays in the 1960s and 1970s in Berlin and elsewhere. These include all the major plays and were published by Faber under the general editorship of James Knowlson. Dougald McMillan and Martha Fehsenfeld's *Beckett in the Theatre* (1988) had already given some idea of Beckett as director, but these notebooks emphatically reveal Beckett's meticulous rehearsal methods and tremendous attention to theatrical shape and form. More significantly they reveal a myriad of telling adjustments and changes that Beckett made to the published texts in bringing his work into realisation on the stage and, hence, raise fundamental questions as to where the 'definitive' text of a Beckett play can now be found.

Archival studies of Beckett have never gone away, even in the headiest days of post-structuralist theory. This sort of scholarly research gives ballast to the more interpretative and theoretical work that has appeared alongside it and may well prove more enduring. These studies, and the contextual interests that support them, imbued the study of Beckett with scholarly rigour and have set a standard of excellence for the empirical mapping of Beckett's artistic career. Indeed, since the theory wars that animated English studies a generation ago have now stilled somewhat or the theoretical reverberations have now been absorbed into general practice, there has been something of a surge in archival or empirical Beckett studies in recent years. If the awareness of history and context discernible in theorised Beckett criticism of the 1990s can continue to connect with the empirical advances of professional Beckett scholarship, it promises a rich future for academic Beckett studies.

Notes

Introduction

1. Samuel Beckett, quoted by Colin Duckworth, 'Introduction', Samuel Beckett, *En Attendant Godot*, ed. Colin C. Duckworth (London: George C. Harrap, 1966), p. xxv.
2. Beckett to Tom Driver, 'Beckett by the Madeleine', *Columbia University Forum* 4 (Summer, 1961), reprinted in Lawrence Graver and Raymond Federman (eds.), *Samuel Beckett: The Critical Heritage* (London, Henley and Boston: Routledge and Kegan Paul, 1979), p. 220.

1 Beckett's life

1. James Knowlson, *Damned to Fame: The Life of Samuel Beckett* (London: Bloomsbury, 1996), p. xxi.
2. John Pilling's *Beckett Before Godot: The Formative Years, 1929–1946* (Cambridge: Cambridge University Press, 1998) gives a scholarly appraisal of many of these correspondences.
3. Stan Gontarski, *The Intent of Undoing in Samuel Beckett's Dramatic Texts* (Bloomington: Indiana University Press, 1985).
4. Knowlson, *Damned to Fame*, p. 178.
5. Knowlson, *Damned to Fame*, p. 180.
6. Interview with Tom Driver, 'Beckett by the Madeleine', *Columbia University Forum* 4 (Summer, 1961), in Graver and Federman, *Samuel Beckett: The Critical Heritage*, p. 220.
7. Deirdre Bair, *Samuel Beckett: A Biography* (London: Jonathan Cape, 1978), p. 14.
8. Vivian Mercier, *Beckett/Beckett* (Oxford: Oxford University Press, 1977), p. 26.
9. Andrew Kennedy, *Samuel Beckett* (Cambridge: Cambridge University Press, 1989), p. 4.
10. Knowlson, *Damned to Fame*, p. 78.
11. Ibid., p. 105.

12. Ibid., p. 160.
13. Ibid., p. 126.
14. Ibid., p. 126.
15. Ibid., p. 163.
16. Ibid., p. 171.
17. Ibid., p. 273.
18. Ibid., p. 282.
19. Ibid., p. 304.
20. Linda Ben-Zvi, *Samuel Beckett* (Boston: Twayne, 1986), p. 16.
21. Interview with Gabriel d'Aubarède (1961), trans. Christopher Waters, in Graver and Federman, *Samuel Beckett: The Critical Heritage*, p. 217.
22. Interview with Israel Shenker (1956), in Graver and Federmen, p. 148.
23. Knowlson, *Damned to Fame*, pp. 359, 355.
24. Quoted in Knowlson., p. 414.
25. Anthony Cronin, *Samuel Beckett: The Last Modernist* (London: Harper Collins, 1996), p. 416.
26. Ibid., p. 501.
27. Billie Whitelaw, *Billie Whitelaw . . . Who He?* (London: Hodder and Stoughton, 1995), p. 80.

2 Cultural and intellectual contexts

1. Interview with Gabriel d'Aubarède, in Graver and Federman, *Samuel Beckett: The Critical Heritage*, p. 217.
2. Arthur Schopenhauer, *The World as Will and Representation*, trans. E. F. J. Payne, 2 vols. (New York: Dover, 1966), I: 325
3. James Knowlson (text) and John Haynes (photographs), *Images of Beckett* (Cambridge: Cambridge University Press, 2003), p. 18.
4. Charles Juliet, 'Meeting Beckett', trans. and ed. Suzanne Chamier, *TriQuarterly* 77 (Winter, 1989–90), p. 17. An extract from *Rencontre avec Samuel Beckett* (Saint-Clément-la-Rivière: Editions Fata Morgana, 1986).
5. Interview with Tom Driver, 'Beckett by the Madeleine', *Columbia University Forum* 4 (Summer, 1961), reprinted in Graver and Federman, *Samuel Beckett: The Critical Heritage*, p. 219.
6. *Transition* 16/17 (Spring–Summer, 1929).
7. Cronin, *Samuel Beckett: The Last Modernist*, p. 494.

3 Plays

1. In a letter to his American publisher, Barney Rosset, quoted in Knowlson, *Damned to Fame*, p. 412.
2. Quoted in Graver and Federman, *Samuel Beckett: The Critical Heritage*, p. 10.
3. Vivian Mercier, 'The Uneventful Event', *Irish Times* (18 February 1956), p. 9.
4. Quoted in James Knowlson and Dougald McMillan (eds.), *The Theatrical Notebooks of Samuel Beckett*, vol. I: *Waiting for Godot* (London: Faber and Faber, 1994), p. xiv.
5. Walter Asmus, 'Beckett Directs Godot', *Theatre Quarterly* 5, 19 (September–November, 1975), p. 21.
6. 'Knook': a deliberately obscure word, with no clear meaning in English, French or German. It is said to have been coined by Beckett by analogy with *knout* (Russian for whip): Knowlson and MacMillan, *Theatrical Notebooks*, vol. I, pp. 121–2.
7. Tom Driver, 'Beckett by the Madeleine', *Columbia University Forum* 4 (Summer, 1961), in Graver and Federman, *Samuel Beckett: The Critical Heritage*, p. 220.
8. Letter to Professor Tom Bishop, 1978. Quoted in Dougald McMillan and Martha Fehsenfeld, *Beckett in the Theatre: The Author as Practical Playwright and Director*, vol. I (London: John Calder, 1988), p. 13.
9. Graver and Federman, *Samuel Beckett: The Critical Heritage*, p. 10.
10. S. E. Gontarski (ed. and notes), *The Theatrical Notebooks of Samuel Beckett*, vol. II: *Endgame* (London: Faber and Faber, 1992), p. 61.
11. Theodor Adorno, 'Towards an Understanding of *Endgame*', trans. Samuel M. Weber, in Bell Gale Chevigny (ed.), *Twentieth-Century Interpretations of 'Endgame'* (Englewood Cliffs, NJ: Prentice-Hall, 1969), p. 84.
12. Knowlson and Haynes, *Images of Beckett*, p. 18.
13. Quoted in Clas Zilliacus, *Beckett and Broadcasting: A Study of the Works of Samuel Beckett for and in Radio and Television* (Åbo: Åbo Akademi, 1976), p. 30.
14. Martin Esslin, 'Beckett and the Art of Broadcasting', *Mediations: Essays on Brecht, Beckett and the Media* (London: Eyre Methuen, 1980), p. 130.
15. Donald McWhinnie, *The Art of the Radio* (London: Faber and Faber, 1959), p. 11.
16. Letter from Samuel Beckett to Barney Rosset, 27 August 1957. Quoted in Zilliacus, *Beckett and Broadcasting*, p. 3.
17. Lawrence Harvey, *Samuel Beckett: Poet and Critic* (Princeton: Princeton University Press, 1970), p. 247.
18. Ibid., p. 248.
19. Knowlson, *Damned to Fame*, p. 176.
20. Charles Juliet, 'Meeting Beckett', *TriQuarterly* 77 (Winter, 1989/90), p. 10.
21. Quoted in Everett C. Frost, 'Fundamental Sounds: Recording Samuel Beckett's Radio Plays', *Theatre Journal* 43, 3 (October, 1991), p. 376.

22. Quoted in Zilliacus, *Beckett and Broadcasting*, p. 83. '*Embers* rests on an ambiguity: is the character having an hallucination or is he in the presence of reality? Stage performance would destroy the ambiguity' (my translation).
23. McMillan and Fehsenfeld, *Beckett in the Theatre*, pp. 288–9.
24. Letter from Samuel Beckett to Alan Schneider, 4 January 1960, in Maurice Harmon (ed.), *No Author Better Served: The Correspondence of Samuel Beckett and Alan Schneider* (Cambridge, MA, and London: Harvard University Press, 1998), p. 60.
25. James Knowlson has explored this dimension in *Light and Darkness in the Theatre of Samuel Beckett* (London: Turret Books, 1972) and James Knowlson (ed.), *The Theatrical Notebooks of Samuel Beckett*, vol. III: *Krapp's Last Tape* (London: Faber and Faber, 1992).
26. Knowlson, *Light and Darkness*, p. 141.
27. Ibid., p. 141.
28. Knowlson and Haynes, *Images of Beckett*, p. 8.
29. Kenner, *A Reader's Guide to Samuel Beckett* (London: Thames and Hudson, 1973), p. 147.
30. From Martha Fehsenfeld's Rehearsal Diary, quoted in James Knowlson (ed.), *Happy Days: The Production Notebook of Samuel Beckett* (London and Boston: Faber and Faber, 1985), p. 177.

4 Prose works

1. Rabin Rabinovitz provides a list of these recurring passages in Appendix I ('Repeated Sentences, Phrases, and Rare Words in *Murphy*') and Appendix II ('Repeated Episodes, Objects and Allusions in *Murphy*') of his *The Development of Samuel Beckett's Fiction* (Urbana: University of Illinois Press, 1984), pp. 185–99 and pp. 200–21.
2. Hugh Kenner was among the first to explore the Cartesian dimension to Beckett's work in *Samuel Beckett: A Critical Study* (London: John Calder, 1962).
3. Samuel Beckett, *Dream of Fair to Middling Women* (Dublin: Black Cat Press, 1992), pp. 119–20.
4. Kenner, *A Reader's Guide to Samuel Beckett*, p. 75.
5. Israel Shenker, 'Interview with Samuel Beckett', *New York Times*, 5 May 1956, p. 3.
6. The picture first appeared publicly in *Beckett at 60* (London: Calder and Boyars, 1967), facing p. 24.
7. Walter Benjamin, 'Theses on the Philosophy of History', in *Illuminations*, trans. Harry Zohn, ed. and intro. Hannah Arendt (London: Jonathan Cape, 1970), p. 258.

5 Beckett criticism

1. Kenner, *Samuel Beckett: A Critical Study*, p. 131.
2. P. J. Murphy et al., *Critique of Beckett Criticism: A Guide to Research in English, French and German* (Columbia, SC: Camden House, 1994), p. 17.
3. Martin Esslin (ed.), *Samuel Beckett: A Collection of Critical Essays* (Englewood Cliffs, NJ: Prentice-Hall, 1965), p. 4.
4. Ibid., p. 14.
5. H. Porter Abbott, *The Author in the Autograph* (Ithaca and London: Cornell University Press, 1996), p. 50.
6. Ibid., pp. 127–48.
7. Phil Baker, *Samuel Beckett and the Mythology of Psychoanalysis* (London: Macmillan, 1997), pp. xviii, xv.
8. David Lloyd, 'Writing in the Shit', in *Anomalous States: Irish Writing and the Post-Colonial Moment* (Durham, NC: Duke University Press, 1993), p. 56.
9. Declan Kiberd, *Inventing Ireland: The Literature of the Modern Nation* (London: Jonathan Cape, 1995), p. 531.

Guide to further reading

There follows a selection of biographical, bibliographical, scholarly and critical studies on Beckett. Beckett has elicited a huge body of criticism, and this list should certainly not be regarded as exhaustive. Only books wholly devoted to Beckett are included. For a critical survey of the major trends in Beckett criticism, see Chapter 5.

Biography

Brater, Enoch. *Why Beckett.* London: Thames and Hudson, 1989. A brief introductory literary biography with extensive illustrations.

Cronin, Anthony. *Samuel Beckett: The Last Modernist.* London: HarperCollins, 1996. Eloquently written and informative. Especially strong on Beckett's Irish background.

Gordon, Lois. *The World of Samuel Beckett 1906–1946.* New Haven: Yale University Press, 1996. Emphasises the historical context of Beckett's artistic genesis.

Harmon, Maurice (ed.). *No Author Better Served: The Correspondence of Samuel Beckett and Alan Schneider.* Cambridge, MA, and London: Harvard University Press, 1998. Beckett's correspondence with his American director. The first full-book publication of Beckett's letters. Excludes any material not directly related to the work.

Knowlson, James. *Damned to Fame: The Life of Samuel Beckett.* London: Bloomsbury, 1996. The authorised biography. Comprehensive and indispensable.

Bibliography

Federman, Raymond and John Fletcher. *Samuel Beckett: His Works and His Critics.* Berkeley, Los Angeles and London: University of California Press, 1970. A pioneering survey of the first generation of Beckett criticism.

Murphy, P. J. et. al. *Critique of Beckett Criticism: A Guide to Research in English, French and German.* Columbia, SC: Camden House, 1994. Formidable and comprehensive. Gives an evaluative history of Beckett criticism. Includes a year-by-year bibliography.

Oppenheim, Lois (ed.). *Palgrave Advances in Samuel Beckett Studies.* Basingstoke and New York: Palgrave Macmillan, 2004. A collection of thematic essays by leading Beckettians summarising and evaluating various critical trends.

Critical and Scholarly Studies

Abbott, H. Porter. *Beckett Writing Beckett: The Author in the Autograph.* Ithaca: Cornell University Press, 1996. Elaborates a theory of 'autography', a mode of writing which generates selfhood between autobiography and fiction.

Acheson, James and Kateryna Arthur (eds.). *Beckett's Later Fiction and Drama: Texts for Company.* London: Macmillan, 1987. Useful collection of essays on the later works.

Alvarez, A. *Samuel Beckett.* London: Fontana, 1973. Part of the Fontana Modern Masters series. Well-written introduction.

Baker, Phil. *Samuel Beckett and the Mythology of Psychoanalysis.* London: Macmillan, 1997. Historically locates the psychoanalytical influences on Beckett.

Barge, Laura. *God, the Quest, the Hero: Thematic Structures in Beckett's Fiction.* Chapel Hill: University of North Carolina Press, 1988. Traces the 'God-idea' as thematic and structural influence. Especially notable on Gnostic and Manichaean dimensions.

Begam, Richard. *Samuel Beckett and the End of Modernity.* Stanford: Stanford University Press, 1996. Historically situates the debate about Beckett's position in modernity and postmodernity.

Ben-Zvi, Linda. *Samuel Beckett.* Boston: Twayne, 1986. An introductory survey covering all the work.

Bradby, David. *Beckett: 'Waiting for Godot'. Plays in Production.* Cambridge: Cambridge University Press, 2001. Part of an innovative series looking at the history of production of key plays.

Brater, Enoch. *Beyond Minimalism: Beckett's Late Style in the Theatre.* New York: Oxford University Press, 1987.

The Drama in the Text: Beckett's Late Fiction. New York: Oxford University Press, 1994. Both key studies of the later works.

Bryden, Mary. *Women in Samuel Beckett's Fiction and Drama: Her Own Other.* London: Macmillan, 1993. Theoretical investigation of representations of women in Beckett.

Samuel Beckett and the Idea of God. Basingstoke: Macmillan, 1998. A judicious assessment of religious overtones and their significance.

Cohn, Ruby. *A Beckett Canon.* Ann Arbor: University of Michigan Press, 2001. An indispensable and learned overview of the entire Beckett corpus, across all genres, drawing on a lifetime's scholarship. Cohn has published vastly on Beckett for over forty years.

Connor, Steven (ed.). *Samuel Beckett: Repetition, Theory and Text.* Oxford: Blackwell, 1992. An important contribution to Beckett and post-structuralism, focusing on the function of repetition in Beckett's work.

'*Waiting for Godot*' *and* '*Endgame*'. New Casebooks. New York: St Martin's Press, 1992. Brings together eleven theoretically informed essays.

Doll, Mary. *Beckett and Myth: An Archetypal Approach.* Syracuse: Syracuse University Press, 1988. A Jungian reading strongly informed by postmodern theory.

Esslin, Martin (ed.). *Samuel Beckett: A Collection of Critical Essays.* Englewood Cliffs, NJ: Prentice-Hall, 1965. A highly influential early collection of critical essays.

Fletcher, John. *Samuel Beckett: Waiting for Godot, Krapp's Last Tape and Endgame.* London: Faber and Faber, 2000. A useful annotated commentary on these three major plays.

Friedman, Alan et al. (eds.). *Beckett Translating/Translating Beckett.* University Park: Pennsylvania University Press, 1987. Collection of essays on the important topic of translation.

Gontarski, S. E. *The Intent of Undoing in Samuel Beckett's Dramatic Texts.* Bloomington: Indiana University Press, 1985. A key scholarly work on the evolution of Beckett's dramatic manuscripts.

Graver, Lawrence and Raymond Federman (eds.). *Samuel Beckett: The Critical Heritage.* London, Henley and Boston: Routledge and Kegan Paul, 1979. A very useful anthology of contemporary reviews and criticism of Beckett's works, including reproductions of some of his rare interviews.

Harrington, John P. *The Irish Beckett.* Syracuse: Syracuse University Press, 1991. One of the few full-length treatments of the Irish allusions especially in the early prose.

Harvey, Lawrence. *Samuel Beckett: Poet and Critic.* Princeton: Princeton University Press, 1970. A key text in Beckett criticism, not least because of the unusual cooperation given by Beckett himself. The extended treatment of Beckett's poetry especially valuable.

Hesla, David. *The Shape of Chaos: An Interpretation of the Art of Samuel Beckett.* Minneapolis: University of Minnesota Press, 1971. An in-depth philosophical study.

Kalb, Jonathan. *Beckett in Performance.* Cambridge: Cambridge University Press, 1989. Addresses Beckett's plays from the point of view of staging and performance, drawing on personal experience as a director and several interviews with theatre professionals.

Kenner, Hugh. *Samuel Beckett: A Critical Study.* London: John Calder, 1962. Possibly the most influential early study, especially on the Cartesian influences on Beckett. Well written and still engaging.

Knowlson, James. *Light and Darkness in the Theatre of Samuel Beckett.* London: Turret Books, 1972. Treats dualism and the Manichaean dimension.

(ed.). *Happy Days: The Production Notebook of Samuel Beckett.* London and Boston: Faber and Faber, 1985. A precursor to the series of theatrical notebooks published under Knowlson's general editorship.

Knowlson, James and John Pilling. *Frescoes of the Skull: The Later Prose and Drama of Samuel Beckett.* London: John Calder, 1979. Pioneering study of the later Beckett, with some treatment of earlier, then unpublished works like *Eleutheria.*

Knowlson, James and Dougald McMillan (eds.). *The Theatrical Notebooks of Samuel Beckett,* vol. I: *Waiting for Godot.* London: Faber and Faber, 1994. Part of a valuable series publishing and annotating the various production notebooks Beckett kept while directing his plays. See also vol. III on *Krapp's Last Tape,* 1992. S. E. Gontarski edited vol. II: *Endgame,* 1992 and vol. IV: *The Shorter Plays,* 1999.

Locatelli, Carla. *Unwording the Word: Samuel Beckett's Prose Works after the Nobel Prize.* Philadelphia: University of Philadelphia Press, 1990. Challenging analysis of semiotics and representation in Beckett, influenced by deconstruction.

McMillan, Dougald and Martha Fehsenfeld. *Beckett in the Theatre,* vol. I: *The Author as Practical Playwright and Director.* London: John Calder, 1988. Rigorous account of Beckett's practice in the theatre.

McMullan, Anna. *Theatre on Trial: Samuel Beckett's Later Drama.* London: Routledge, 1993. Very useful study of Beckett's later drama informed by various critical theories.

Murphy, P. J. *Reconstructing Beckett: Language for Being in Samuel Beckett's Fiction.* Toronto: Toronto University Press, 1990. Challenges orthodox critical understanding by positing a complex 'realism' and moral seriousness in Beckett's prose. Detailed and enlightening on post-trilogy prose.

O'Brien, Eoin. *The Beckett Country: Samuel Beckett's Ireland.* Dublin: Black Cat Press, 1992. A collection of photographs of the Irish landscape that inspired many of Beckett's works. Introduction by James Knowlson.

Oppenheim, Lois. *The Painted Word: Beckett's Dialogue With Art.* Ann Arbor: University of Michigan Press, 2000. Deals with Beckett's relationship with visual arts and his general intellectual context.

(ed.). *Samuel Beckett and the Arts: Music, Visual Arts and Non-Print Media.* New York: Garland, 1998. A pioneering collection of essays in this important field.

Pilling, John. *Samuel Beckett.* London: Routledge and Kegan Paul, 1976. Especially good on the cultural and intellectual contexts.

Beckett Before Godot: The Formative Years, 1929–1946. Cambridge: Cambridge University Press, 1998. Authoritative and learned treatment of Beckett's early work and influences.

(ed.). *The Cambridge Companion to Samuel Beckett.* Cambridge: Cambridge University Press, 1994. A useful collection of essays on various aspects of Beckett's work. Treats the whole oeuvre.

Pountney, Rosemary. *Theatre of Shadows: Samuel Beckett's Drama 1956–76* (Gerrards Cross: Colin Smythe; Totowa, New Jersey: Barnes and Noble, 1988). A judicious, scholarly and thorough investigation of the drama of this period with rich use of manuscript material.

Ricks, Christopher. *Beckett's Dying Words.* Oxford: Oxford University Press, 1993. Based on his 1990 Clarendon lectures delivered at Oxford University, Ricks argues that Beckett's works are marked by a longing for death and oblivion.

States, Bert O. *The Shape of Paradox: An Essay on Waiting for Godot.* Berkeley: University of California Press, 1978. Excellent formalist reading of the play, alert to the Edenic overtones.

Sussman, Henry and Christopher Devenney (eds.). *Engagement and Indifference: Beckett and the Political.* New York: State University of New York Press, 2001. An edited collection which looks at the political and ethical dimensions to Beckett from a variety of critical approaches.

Trezise, Thomas. *Into the Breach: Samuel Beckett and the Ends of Literature.* Princeton: Princeton University Press, 1990. Early deconstructive study refuting the phenomenological bias of earlier criticism.

Uhlmann, Anthony. *Beckett and Poststructuralism.* Cambridge: Cambridge University Press, 1999. Draws on French philosophers including Derrida, Foucault, Deleuze and Guattari.

Watson, David. *Paradox and Desire in Samuel Beckett's Fiction.* London: Macmillan, 1991. Draws on Lacanian theory and post-structuralism.

Worth, Katherine. *Samuel Beckett's Theatre: Life-Journeys.* Oxford: Oxford University Press, 1999. A highly readable, personal account of working on Beckett from a scholar who has also directed Beckett's plays in the theatre.

Zilliacus, Clas. *Beckett and Broadcasting: A Study of the Works of Samuel Beckett for and in Radio and Television.* Åbo Akademi, 1976. Authoritative and scholarly treatment of Beckett's work in radio and television.

Index